I0020754

Microsoft Dynamics 365 Lean

A complete review of the essential setups needed to implement D365 Lean

Andrew F. Weber

Copyright © 2018 by the Author

All rights reserved.

No part of this publication may be reproduced, stored in a retrieval system or transmitted in any form or by any means without the prior written permission of the author.

ISBN-13: 978-1725622456
ISBN-10: 1725622459

Table of Contents

Introduction

This is a D365 lean module essentials handbook. All basic and requisite setups, with typical transaction examples, are included. The document assumes knowledge of the following:

Item and bom setup

Master planning

Financial setups and dimensions

No advanced warehousing setups are used in the examples. Discrete planning and Sub-contracting setups are not covered in this document.

Setup explanations and field input recommendations precede each screen copy. Data inputs and nomenclature can be found on the screen copies. If a field is not mentioned, it is not needed for that setup example. The table of contents is also a setup sequence summary.

About the Author: Mr. Weber is an AX and D365 developer and implementer. He can be reached at AndrewFWeber@gmail.com

Product version: Microsoft Dynamics 365 for Finance and Operations (8.0)

Platform version: Update 15

Production Parameters, Lean

Note: Instructions precede screen copies

1. Go to Production control > Setup > Production control parameters.

2. Click the Lean manufacturing tab.

3. Input

    1. Production instruction default

        1. 'File' or 'Note' is typically used

        2. If supplemental document print outs are required with Kanbans, print management updates will be required (print management is not covered in this document)

    2. Quantity unit of measure default

        1. Note: if used, 'ea' may need a unit measure update

    3. Time unit of measure default

4. Split ledger, ignore

5. Batch Processing, ignore (process manufacturing is not covered in this document)

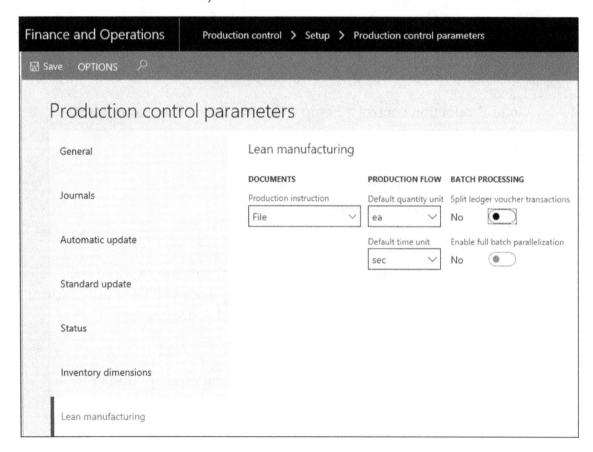

Production Flow Models

Note: Instructions precede screen copies

1. Go to Production control > Setup > Lean production flow > Production flow models.

2. Click New.

3. In the Production flow model field, type a value.

4. In the Model type field, select an option.

5. In the Planning period type field, select an option.

6. In the Planning time fence field, enter a number.

7. In the Capacity shortage reaction field, select an option.

8. Close the page.

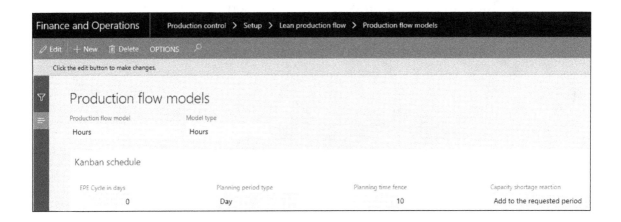

Notes on Production Flow Models:

EPE

- Is a lead time offset that is applied during scheduling

MODEL TYPE

- 'Throughput' schedules and consumes capacity by quantity
- 'Hours' schedules and consumes capacity by time

PLANNING TIME FENCE

- Is the period during which kanban cards can be automatically planned
  - Kanban Rule for auto planning flag setups are not applied outside this fence. (see Kanban Rules section)
  - Kanban schedule board also displays based on this time frame.

CAPACITY SHORTAGE REACTION

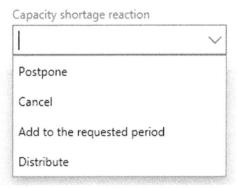

- Postpone full quantity to first available date – finite capacity
- Cancel order if capacity is not available – finite capacity
- Add to Period - **in**finite capacity
- Distribute quantity – finite capacity (typically used)

Work Cells

Note: Instructions precede screen copies

1. Go to Production control > Setup > Resources > Resource groups.

2. Click New.

3. On the General fast tab

4. In the Resource group field, type a value.

5. In the Description field, type a value.

6. In the Site field, enter or select a value.

7. **Select Yes in the Work cell field.**

8. In the Input warehouse field, enter or select a value.

9. In the Input location field, enter or select a value.

10. In the Output warehouse field, enter or select a value.

11. In the Output location field, enter or select a value.

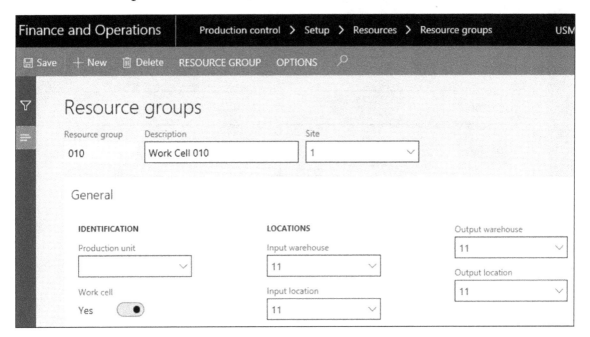

12.   On the Operation fast tab

13.   In the Run time category field, enter or select a value.

    1.   Note, cost category financial setups are not covered in this document

    2.   Setup and Quantity cost categories are <u>not</u> used by Lean

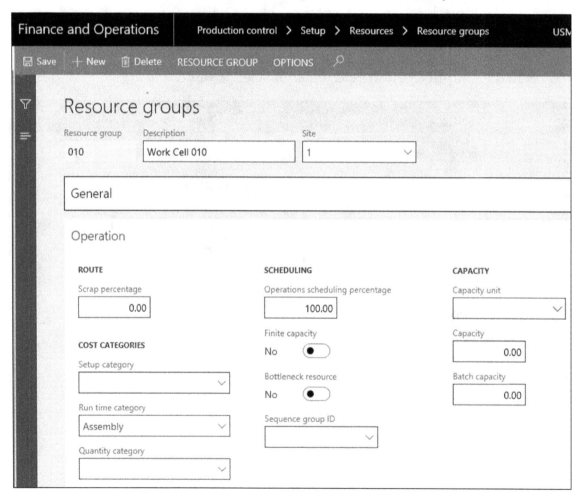

14.   In the Calendar field, enter or select a value.

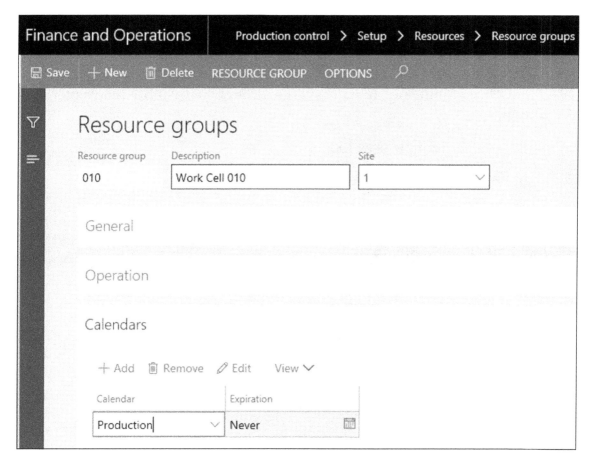

15. On the Work Cell Capacity fast tab

16. In the Production flow model field, enter or select a value.

17. In the Capacity period field, select Throughput or Hours.

    1. This example uses Throughput.

18. Enter capacity period

    1. This example uses standard workday.

19. For Throughput only, in the Average throughput quantity field, enter a number.

    1. This example uses 100.

20. In the Unit field, enter or select a value.

21. Click Save.

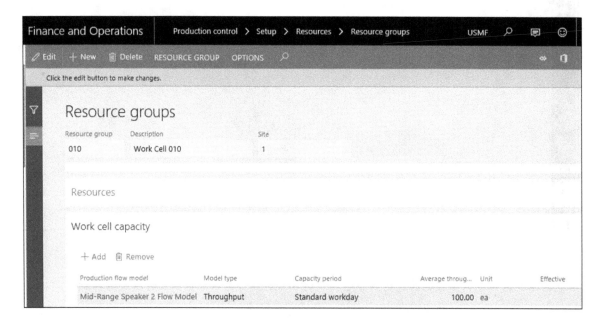

Note, these settings also affect Kanban Schedule board display parameters.

Value Streams

Note: Instructions precede screen copies

1. Go to Production control > Setup > Lean production flow > Value streams.

2. Click New.

3. In the Name field, type a value.

4. Click Save.

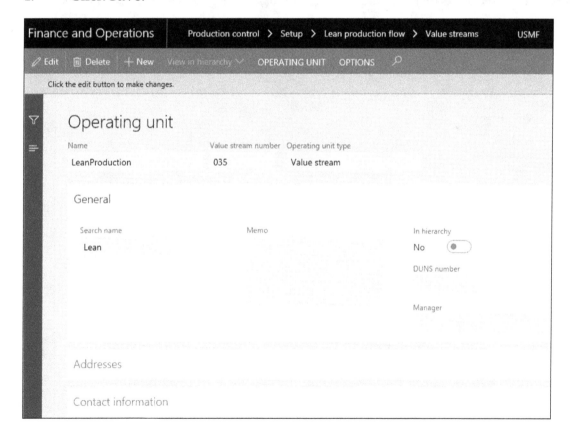

Note: Value streams can be used as a financial dimension.

Production Groups

Note: Instructions precede screen copies

1.   Go to Production control > Setup > Production > Production groups.

    1.   Is part of financial setup, which is not covered in this document.

    2.   Production Groups are used by Production Flows.

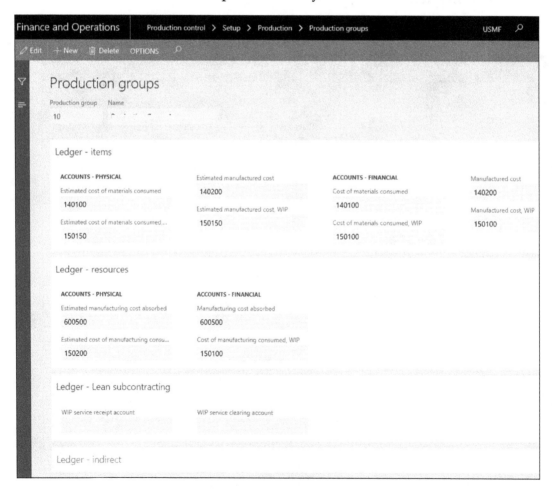

Production Flow Version

Note: Instructions precede screen copies

1. Go to Production control > Setup > Lean production flow > Production flows.

2. Click New.

3. On the General fast tab

4. In the Name field, type a value.

5. In the Description field, type a value.

6. In the Value stream field, enter or select a value.

7. In the Production group field, enter or select a value.

8. Click Save.

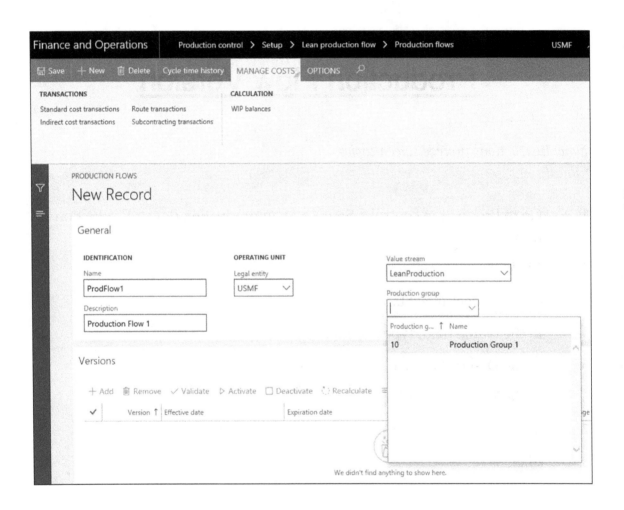

Note: Transactions and the physical voucher can be accessed from the Manage Costs action tab.

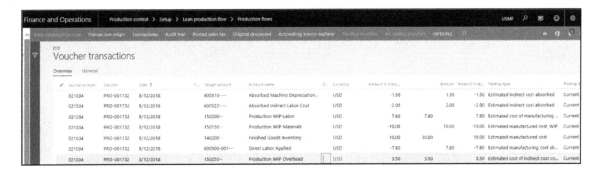

9.   In Versions Click Add.

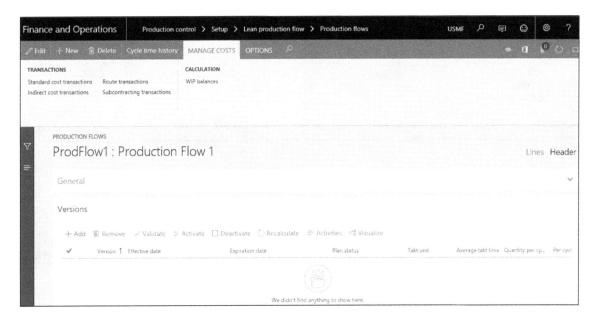

10.   Click OK.

1.   Note, on completion of activities add, Production Flow will need to be activated on the Version fast tab.

11.　Expand the Version Details fast tab.

12.　In the Takt unit field, enter or select a value. (if applicable)

13.　Click Save.

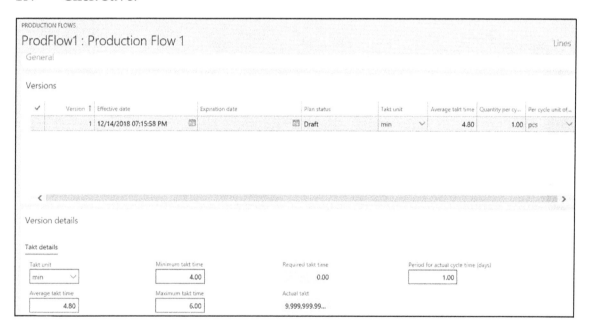

14. Add Financial Dimensions via the 'Header' display option (at right) if applicable (Financial Dimensions setup is not covered in this document)

15. Click Save.

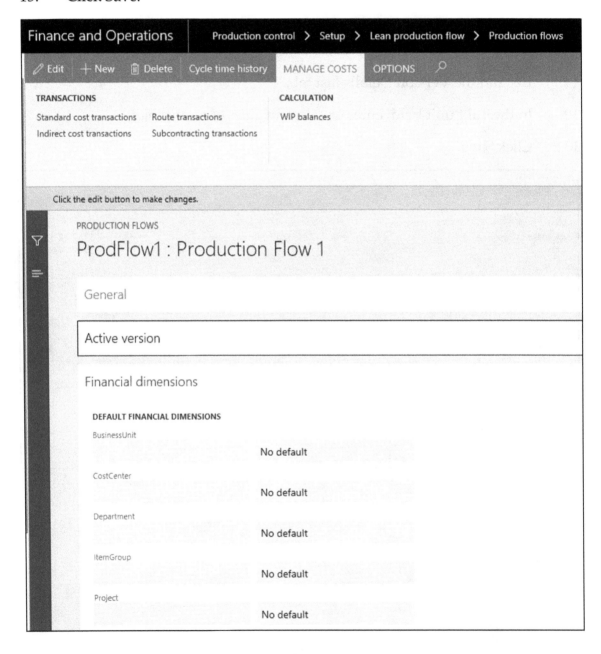

Production Flow Activities - Single

Note: Instructions precede screen copies

1.   From the Versions fast tab action buttons list, click Activities.

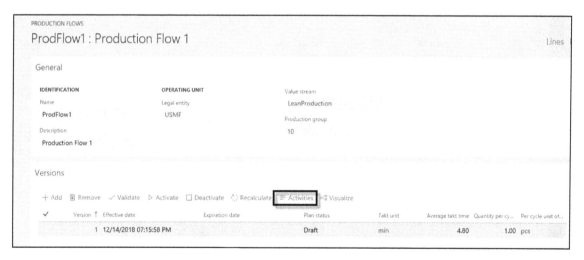

2. Click Create new plan activity.

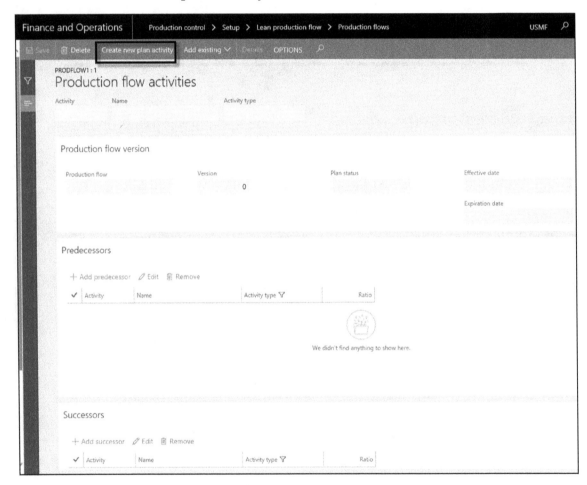

3. Click Next.

4. In the Name field, type a value. (Act1, for Activity 1)

    1. Activities are Lean operations.

5. Click Next.

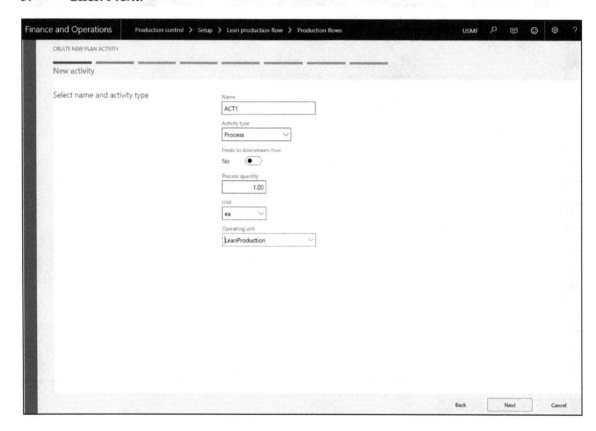

6.   In the Work cell field, enter or select a value.

7.   Click Next.

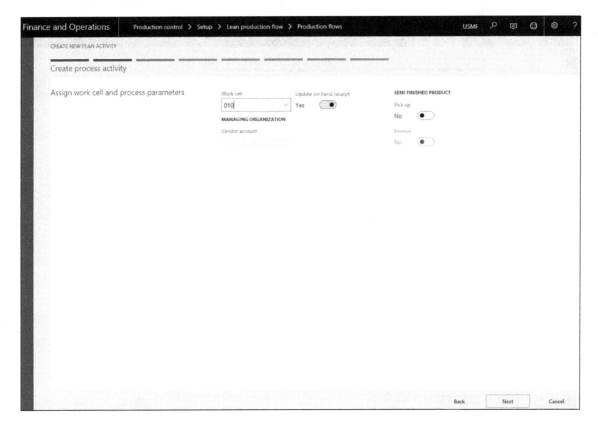

8.   Assign item numbers that need to be manually picked. Otherwise no parts need to be entered, and backflush will automatically consume the bill.

9.   Click Next.

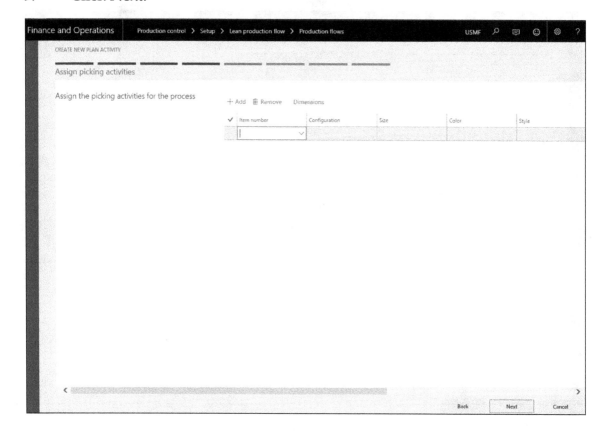

10. Assign a time to the activity. (i.e. time by work cell)

　　1. Times by part, and scheduling display colors, are enabled using Lean Schedule Groups

11. Click Next.

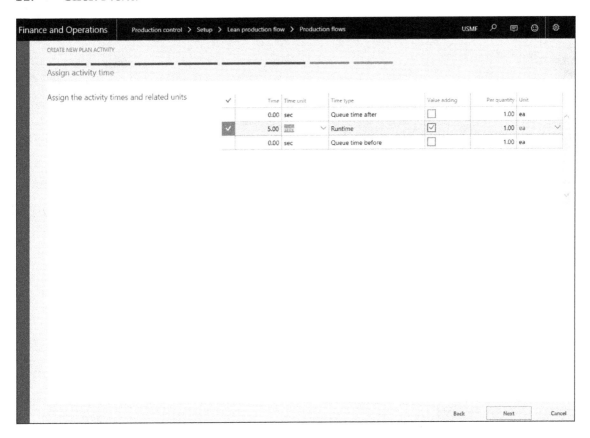

12. Click Finish.

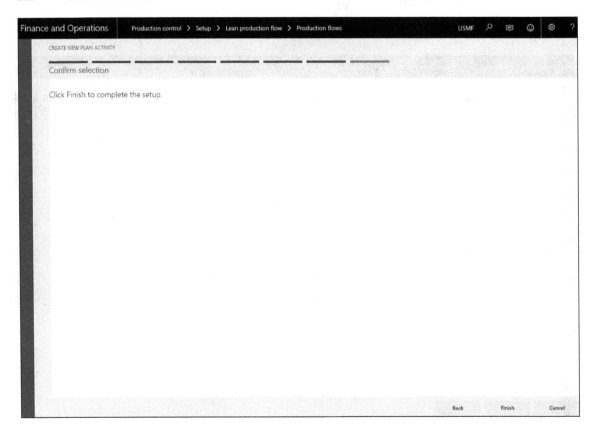

13. Click Save and close the page.

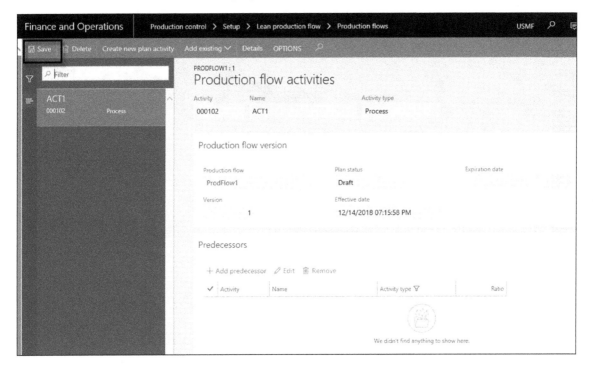

14.   Click Validate. (optional)

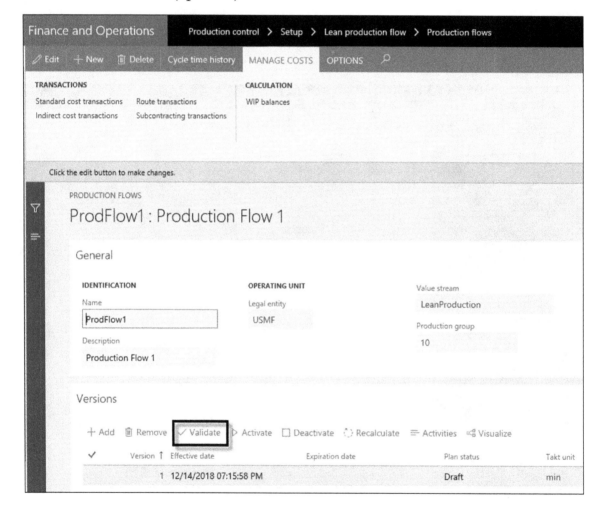

15. Click OK.

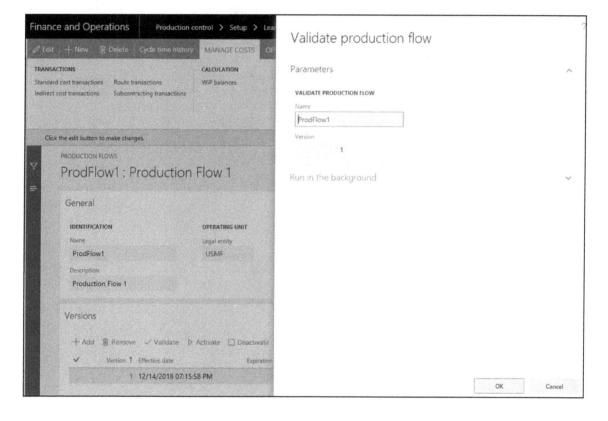

16.   Click Activate.

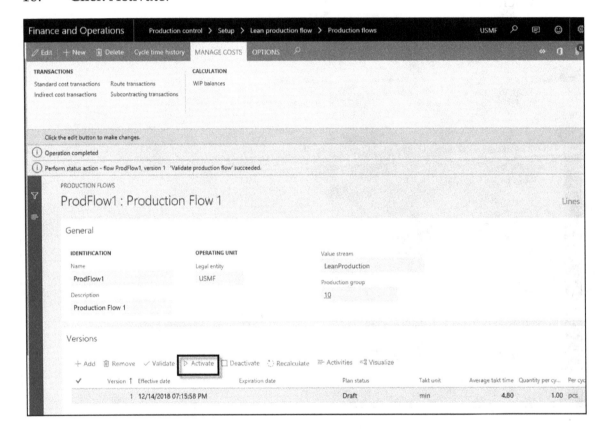

17.   Click OK.

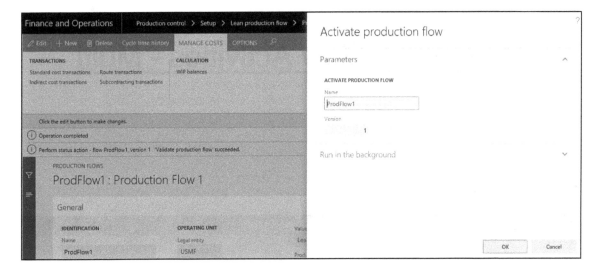

18.   Note Status = Active

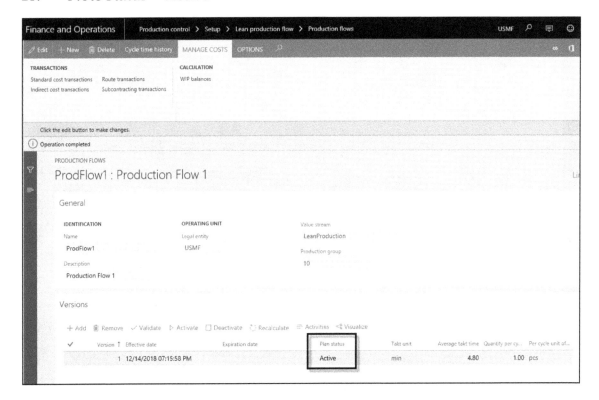

Production Flow Activities - Multi

Note: Instructions precede screen copies

1.   Click Create new plan activity.

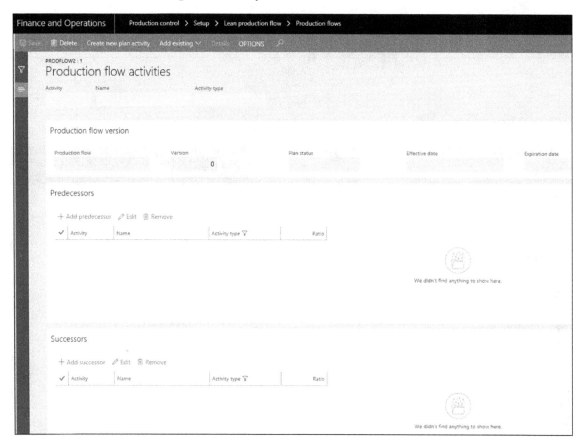

2. Click Next.

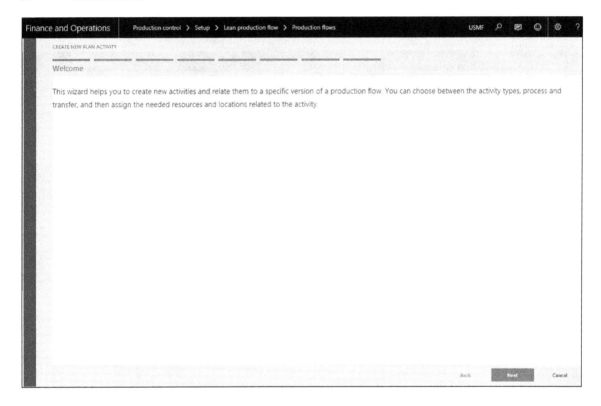

3.   In the Name field, type a value. (Act1)

1.   Activity names can be reused.

4.   Click Next.

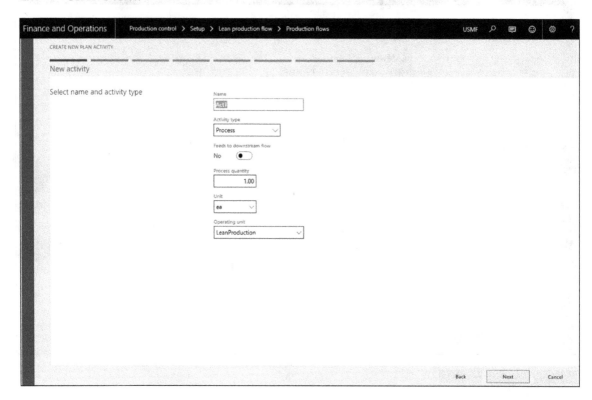

5.   In the Work cell field, enter or select a value.

6.   Select <u>No</u> in the <u>Update on hand</u> receipt field.

   1.   Only the last activity is enabled for Update On Hand

7.   Pick-up is unchanged

8.   Select <u>Yes</u> in the <u>Receive</u> field.

   1.   Product will be sent downstream (i.e. 'received' by the next activity) as semi-finished (i.e. a phantom)

9.   Click Next.

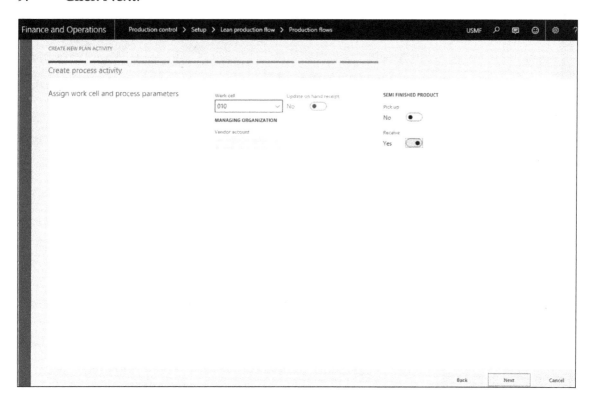

10.   Enter parts that need to be picked manually if applicable. If blank, the bill is flushed automatically.

11.   Click Next.

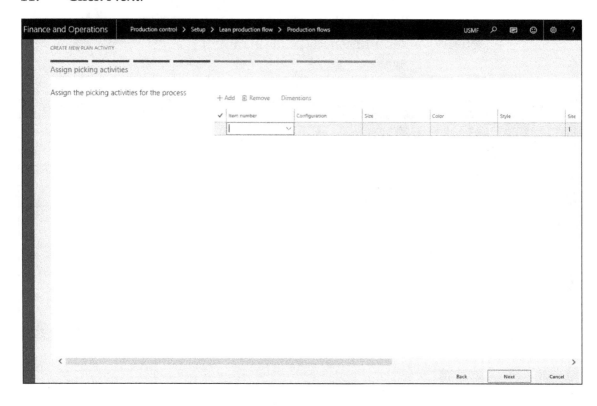

12.	Update Time(s). (i.e. time by work cell)

1.	Times by part are enabled using Lean Schedule Groups

13.	Click Next.

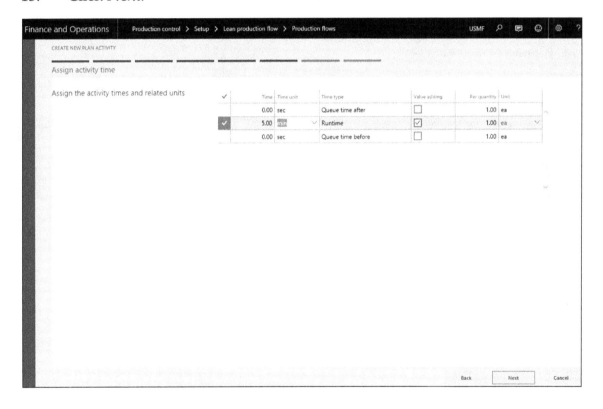

14.   Click Finish.

CREATE NEW PLAN ACTIVITY

Confirm selection

Click Finish to complete the setup.

Back   Finish   Cancel

15. Click Create new plan activity.

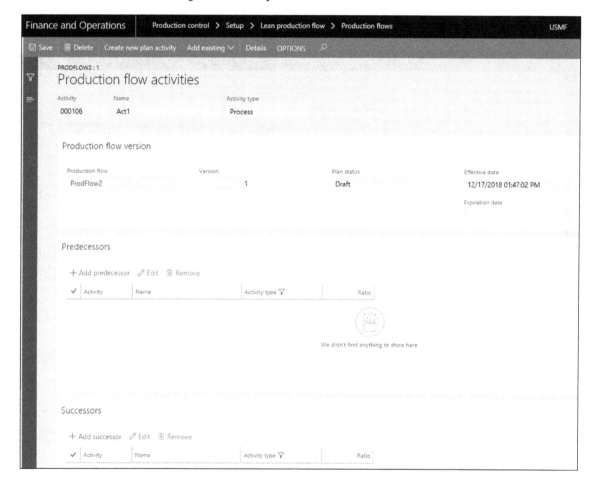

Finance and Operations   Production control > Setup > Lean production flow > Production flows   USMF

Save   🗑 Delete   Create new plan activity   Add existing ∨   Details   OPTIONS   🔎

PRODFLOW2 : 1
Production flow activities

Activity	Name	Activity type
000106	Act1	Process

Production flow version

Production flow	Version	Plan status	Effective date
ProdFlow2	1	Draft	12/17/2018 01:47:02 PM
			Expiration date

Predecessors

+ Add predecessor   ✐ Edit   🗑 Remove

✓	Activity	Name	Activity type ▽	Ratio

We didn't find anything to show here.

Successors

+ Add successor   ✐ Edit   🗑 Remove

✓	Activity	Name	Activity type ▽	Ratio

16.   Click Next.

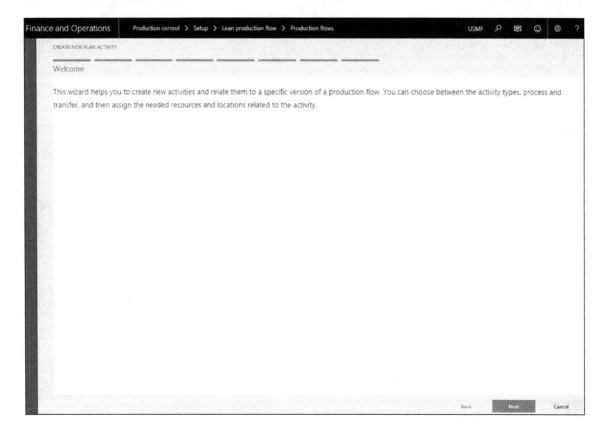

17. In the Name field, type a value. (Act2)

18. Click Next.

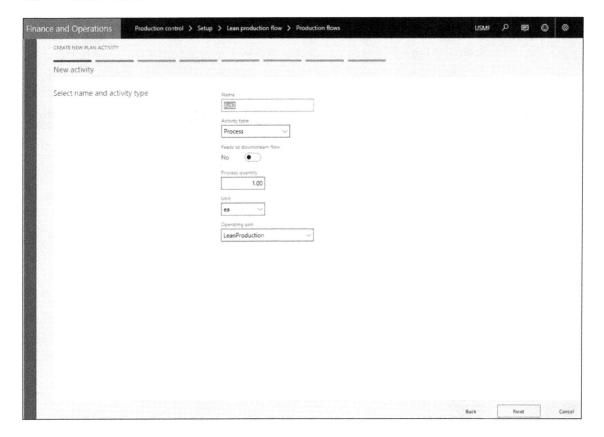

19. In the Work cell field, enter or select a value. (this example uses the same work cell, but typically they would be different)

20. Select No in the Update on hand receipt field.

21. Select Yes in the Pick-up field.

    1. Semi-finished is picked up from upstream activity

22. Select Yes in the Receive field.

    1. Semi-finished is sent to next activity downstream

23. Click Next.

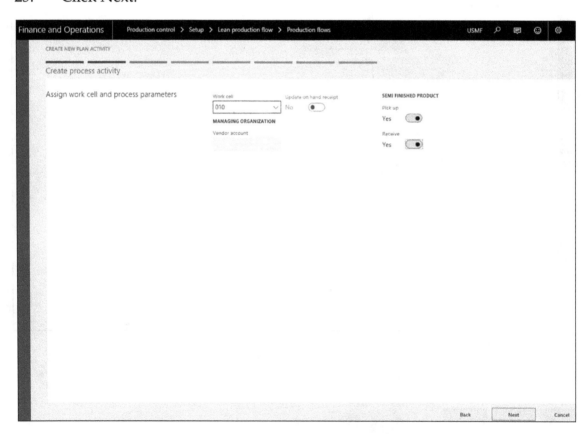

24. Update Time(s) and click Next.

25. Click Next.

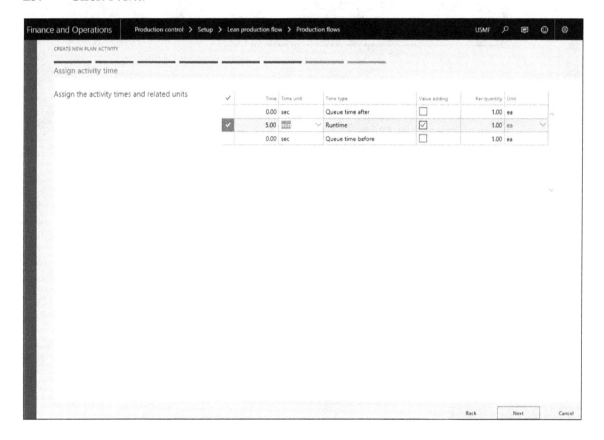

26. Click Finish.

Finance and Operations   Production control > Setup > Lean production flow > Production flows   USMF

CREATE NEW PLAN ACTIVITY

Confirm selection

Click Finish to complete the setup.

Back   Finish   Cancel

27. Click Create new plan activity.

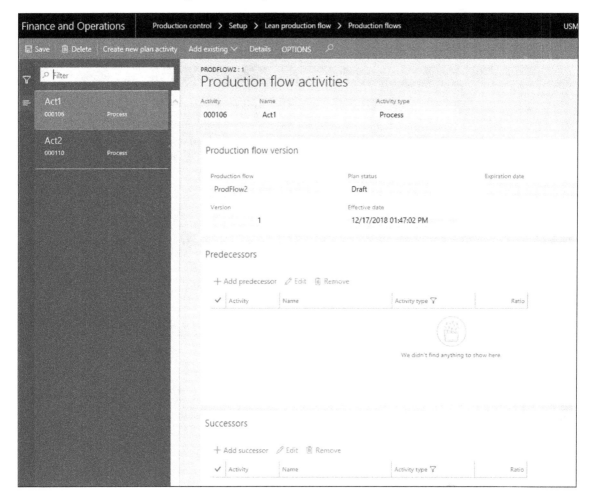

28. Click Next.

29. In the Name field, type a value. (Act3)

30. Click Next.

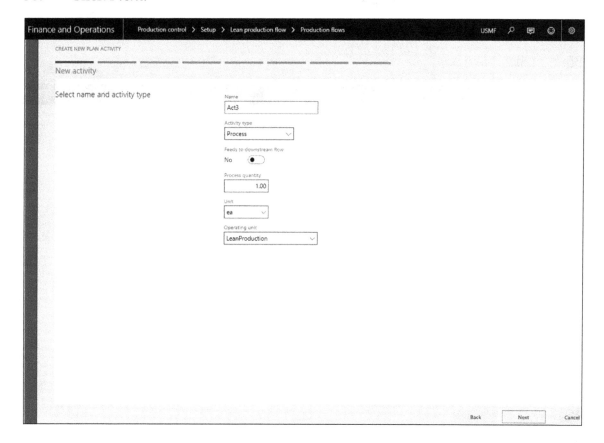

31. In the Work cell field, enter or select a value.

32. Update On Hand is unchanged at Yes.

    1. Act3 is the last activity.

33. Select <u>Yes</u> in the <u>Pick-up</u> field.

34. Receive is unchanged at No – there is nothing to send downstream.

35. Click Next.

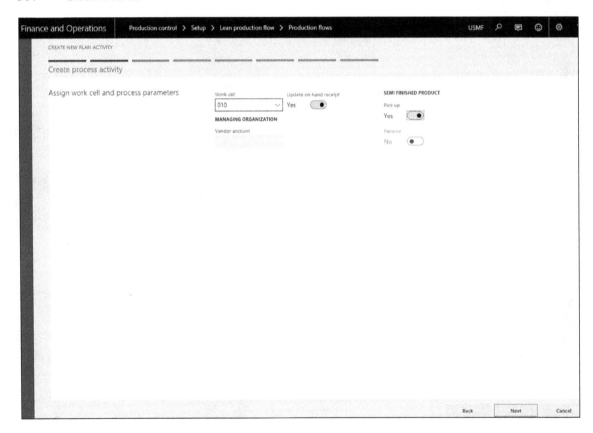

36. Update Time(s).

37. Click Next.

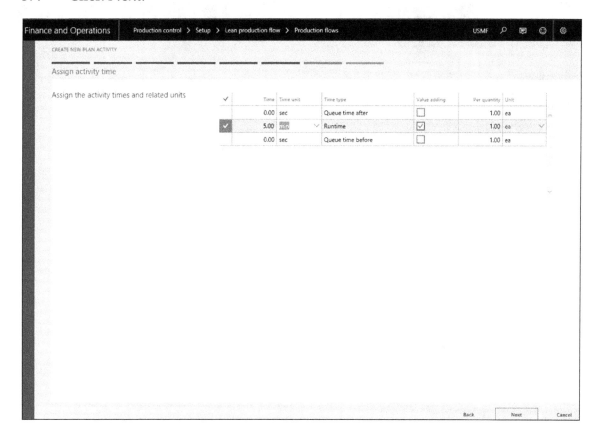

38. Click Finish.

39. Click Add <u>successor</u> for activity 1.

    1. *Predecessor* will be applied automatically for Act2 when setup is completed.

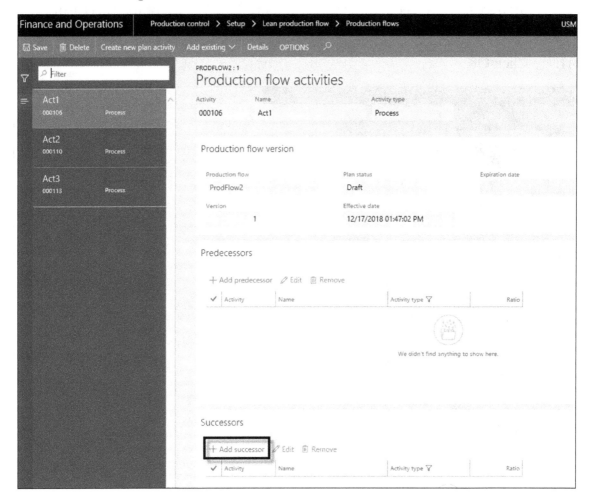

40.   In the Activity field, enter or select a value. (Act2)

1.   In the Cycle time ratio field, enter a number. (how many cycles of the predecessor are needed to supply material for 1 cycle of the successor, typically = 1)

41.   Click OK.

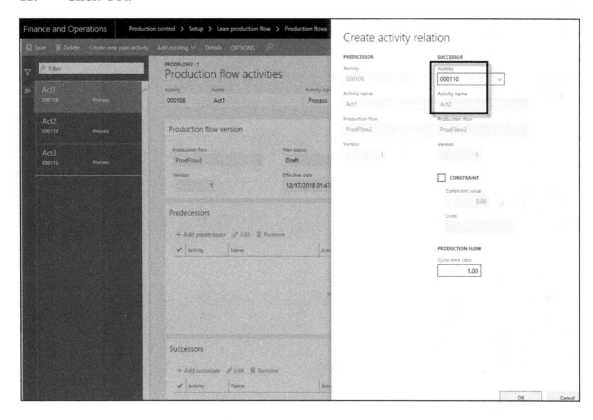

42. Select the second activity. (note activity 1 is listed as a predecessor)

43. Click Add successor.

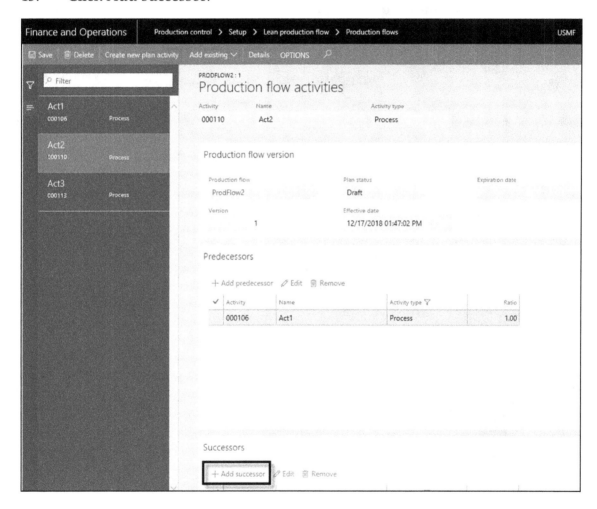

44.	In the Activity field, enter or select a value. (Act3)

45.	In the Cycle time ratio field, enter a number.

46.	Click OK.

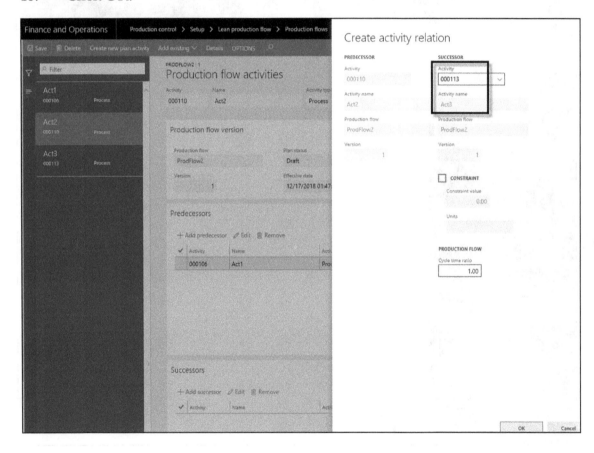

47.   Note that Act2 now has both a predecessor and successor.

48.   Activity 1 and 3 will also show the correct relationship.

49.   Click Save.

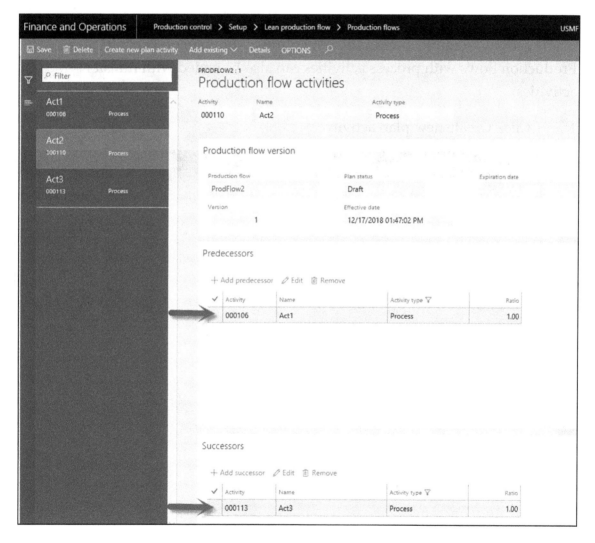

50.   Note that the production flow version will also now require activation.

Production Flow Activities - Transfer

Note: Instructions precede screen copies

Single activity example, defined as a Withdrawal Kanban on kanban rules. Production flows with process activities can also be ended with transfer activities.

1.   Click Create new plan activity.

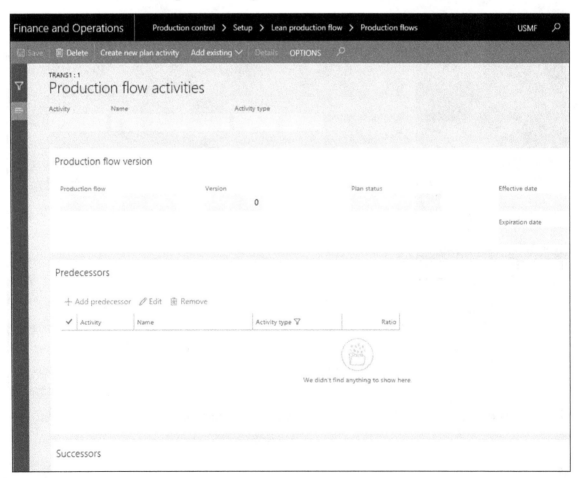

2. Click Next.

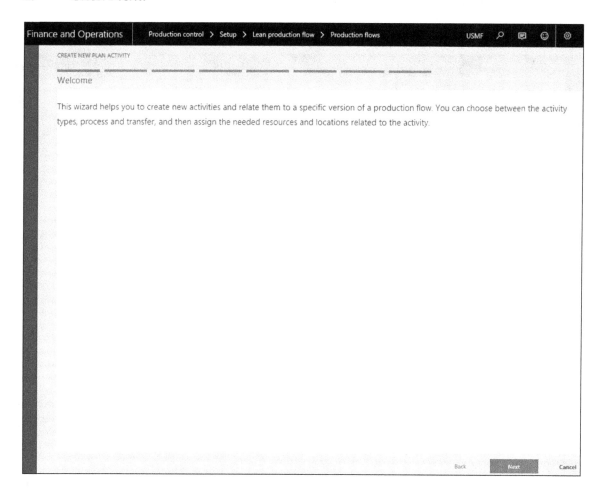

CREATE NEW PLAN ACTIVITY

Welcome

This wizard helps you to create new activities and relate them to a specific version of a production flow. You can choose between the activity types, process and transfer, and then assign the needed resources and locations related to the activity.

Back   Next   Cancel

3. In the Name field, type a value. (ActTrf1)

4. In the Activity type field, select Transfer.

5. Click Next.

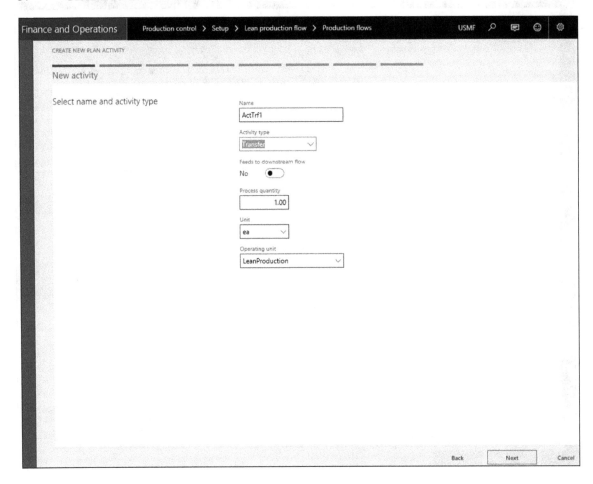

6. Click Next.

1. Use Work Cells if work cell location defaults are needed. Otherwise this setting can be skipped.

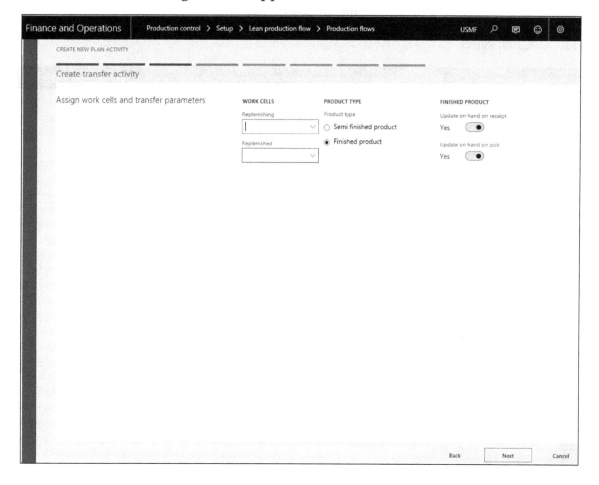

7.   In the Warehouse from field, enter or select a value.

8.   In the Location from field, enter or select a value.

9.   In the Warehouse to field, enter or select a value.

    1.   This example sends the product to a different warehouse.

10.   In the Location to field, enter or select a value.

11.   Click Next.

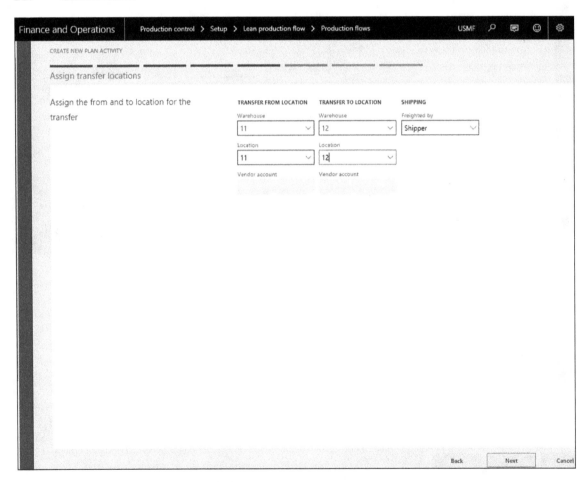

12. In the Time(s) field, enter a number.

13. Click Next.

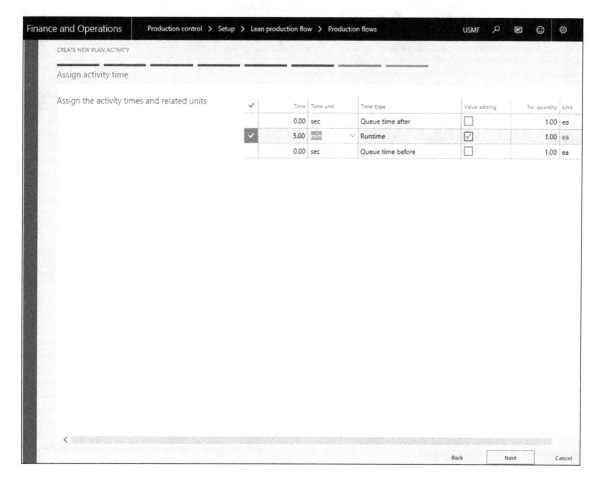

14. Click Finish.

15. Click Save. (Note, Production Flow will need to be activated)

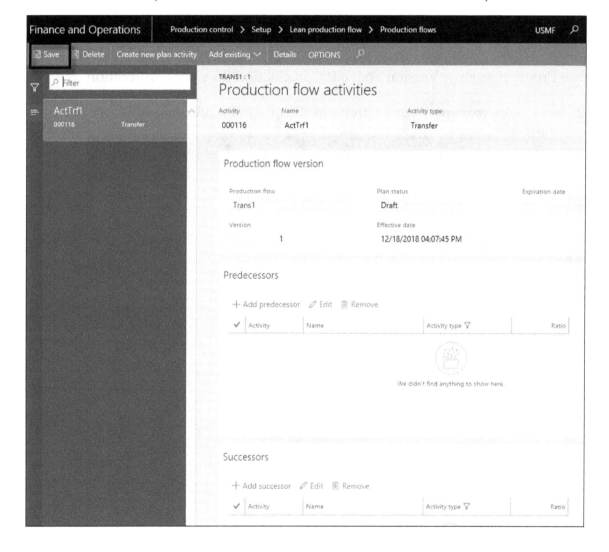

Production Flows - Chained

Note: Instructions precede screen copies

Chained Production Flows are typically used by Sales Event kanbans

See Production Flow Version above for production flow version creation

2.   Click Create new plan activity in the <u>upstream</u> production flow.

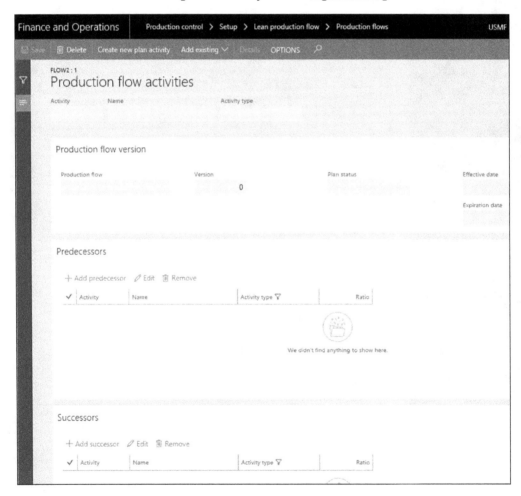

3.   Click Next.

Finance and Operations   Production control > Setup > Lean production flow > Production flows   USMF

CREATE NEW PLAN ACTIVITY

Welcome

This wizard helps you to create new activities and relate them to a specific version of a production flow. You can choose between the activity types, process and transfer, and then assign the needed resources and locations related to the activity.

Back   Next   Cancel

4.　　In the Name field, type a value. (A2)

5.　　Select Yes in the Feeds to downstream flow field.

6.　　Click Next.

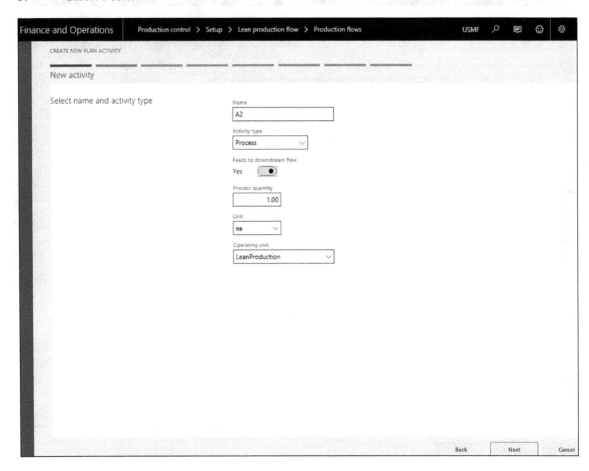

7. In the Work cell field, enter or select a value. (020)

8. Click Next.

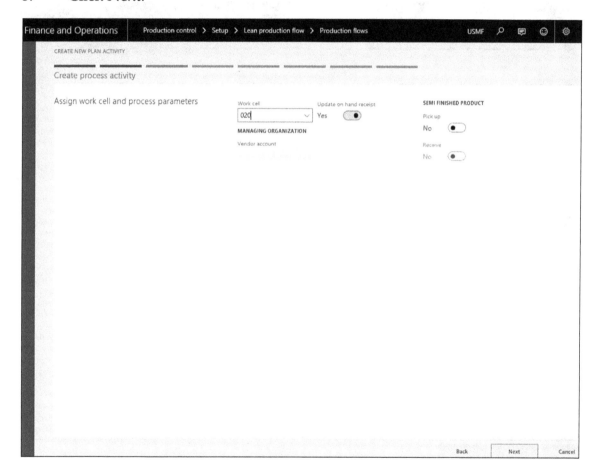

9. Click Next.

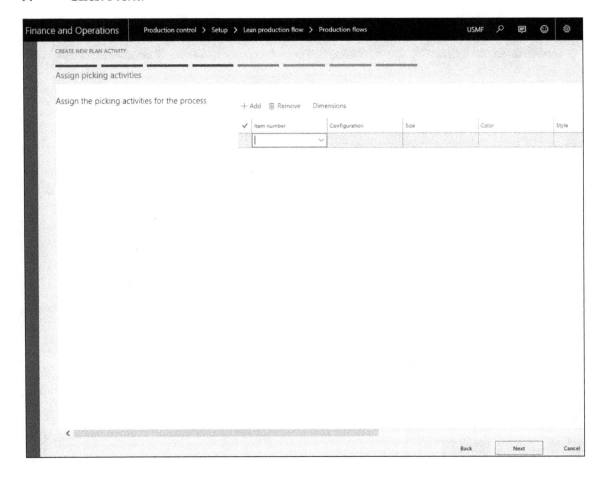

10. Update Time(s).

11. Click Next.

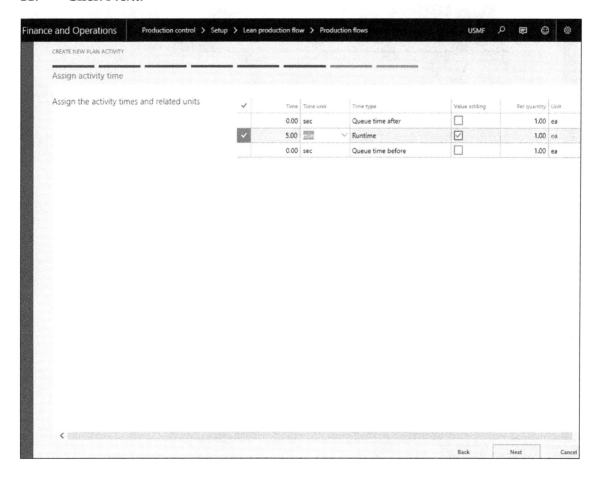

12.   Click Finish.

CREATE NEW PLAN ACTIVITY

Confirm selection

Click Finish to complete the setup.

Back   Finish   Cancel

13. Click Save, close the page, and Activate.

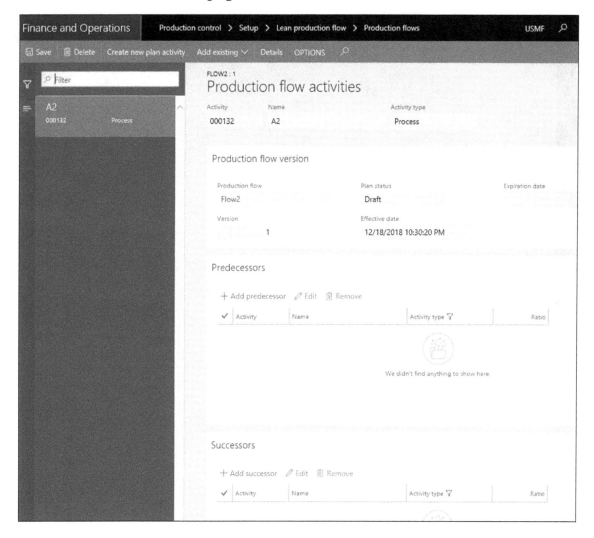

14. Click Create new plan activity in the <u>downstream</u> production flow. In this example Flow2 feeds Flow1.

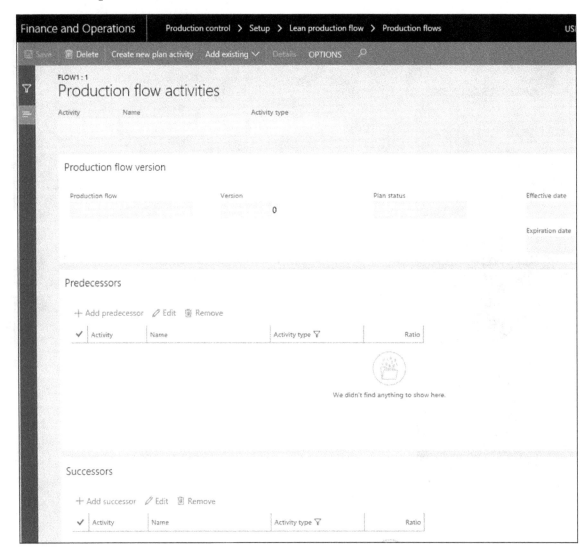

15.   Click Next.

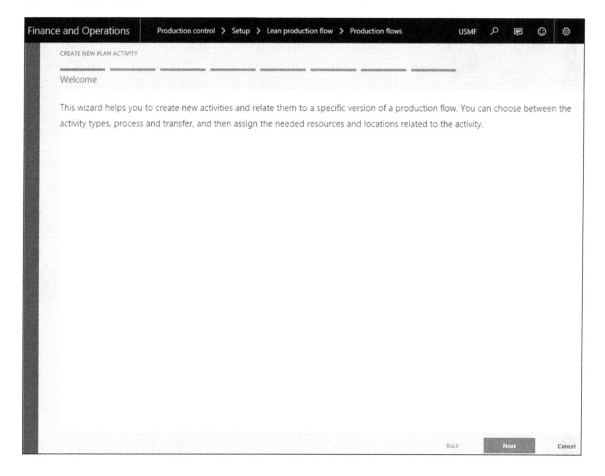

16.   In the Name field, type a value. (A1)

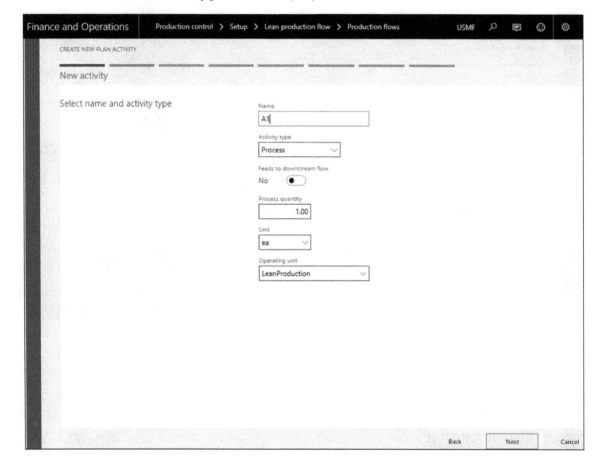

17. In the Work cell field, enter or select a value. (010)

18. Click Next.

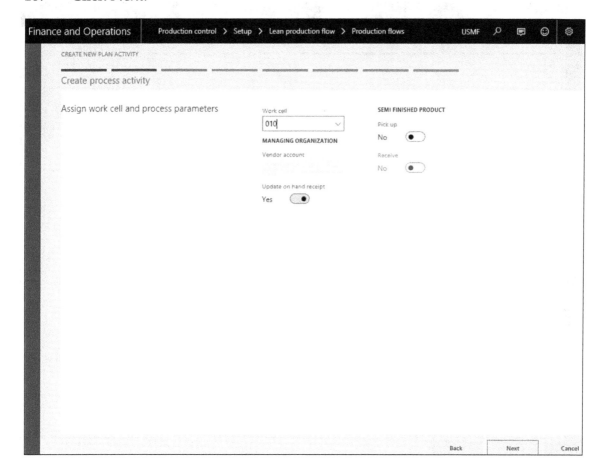

19. Click Next.

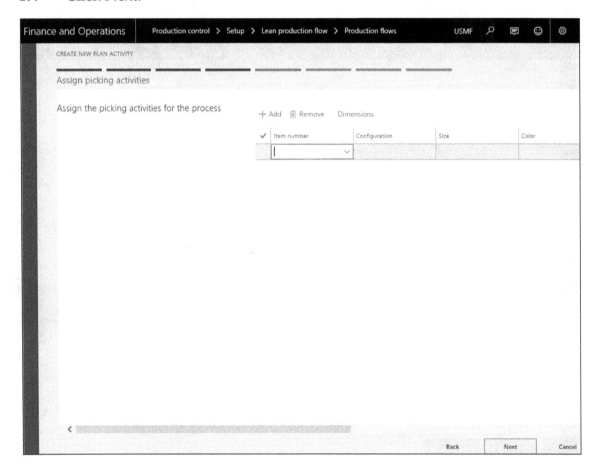

20. Update Time(s).

21. Click Next.

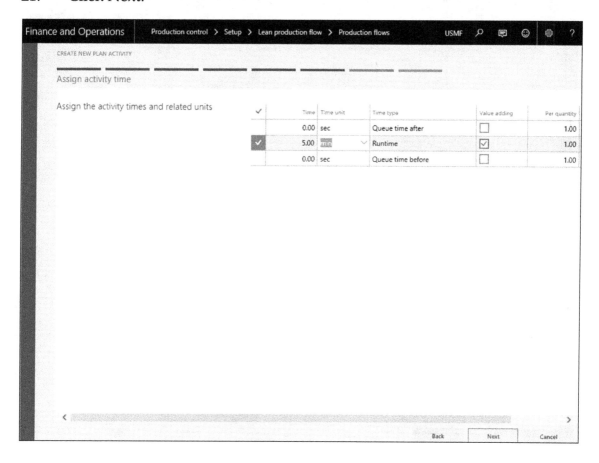

22.   Click Finish.

23. Click Add predecessor.

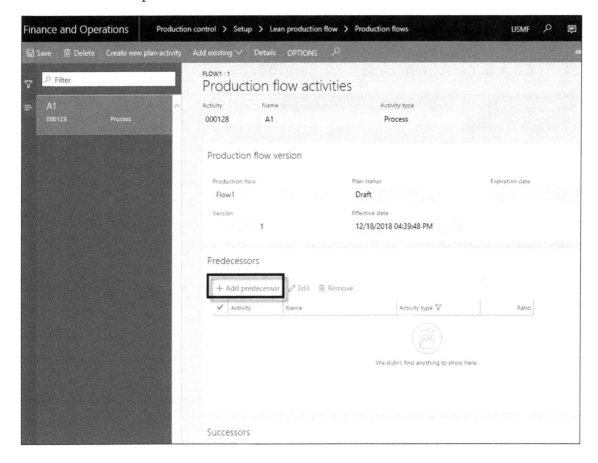

24.   Click in the Activity field.

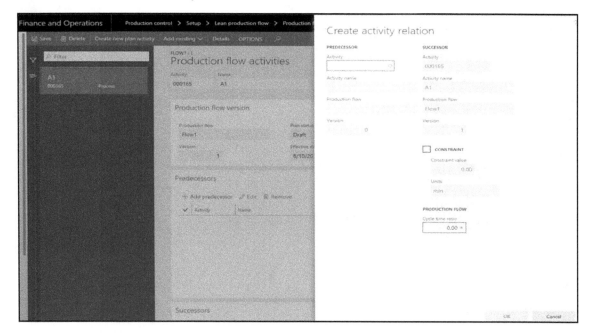

25.   From the Activity pull down, select 'Feeder'.

26.   In the list, select the <u>upstream</u> production flow activity. (Note, this activity is listed because the 'feeds to downstream flow' flag was enabled)

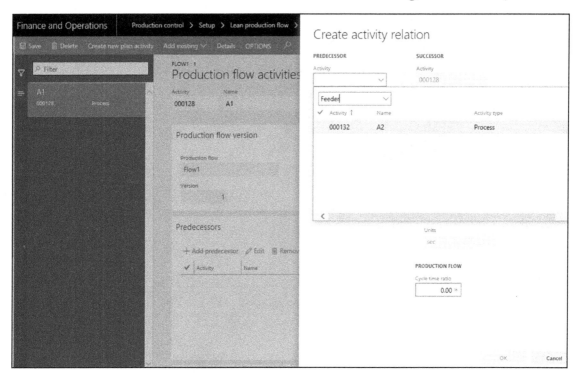

27. In the Cycle time ratio field, enter a number. (how many cycles of the predecessor are needed to supply material for 1 cycle of the successor, typically = 1)

28. Click OK.

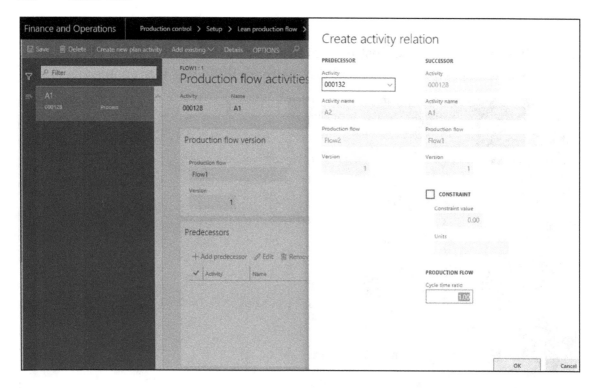

29.   Click Save, close, and activate.

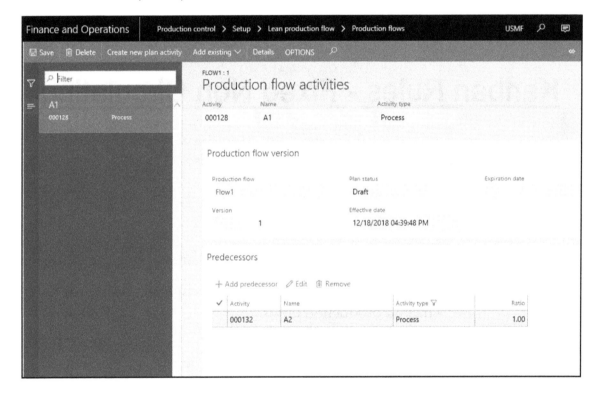

Note, both production flows need to be activated.

Kanban Rules - Fixed Non Circulating

Note: Instructions precede screen copies

1. Click New.

    1. Example uses manufacturing sales event kanban, single activity.

        1. Note, chained kanbans for Sales Event kanbans require chained production flows.

2. **Replenishment type defaults to Fixed**. In the First plan activity field select a value.

   1. Note, if using multiple activity production flow, turn on the multiple activities flag and select the ending activity for multiple activity production flows. A Production Flow path is also defined via this setup step.

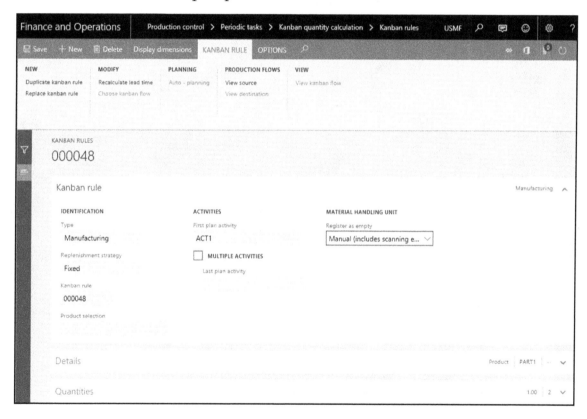

3.   On the Details fast tab in the Product field, apply a product

1.   Product families are not used by Fixed

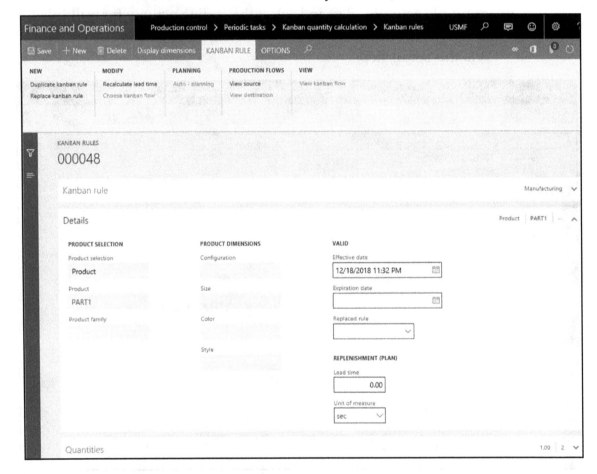

4. On the Quantities fast tab:

    1. In the Default quantity field, enter a number.

    2. In the Fixed kanban (number of cards) quantity field, enter a number.

    3. In the Automatic planning quantity field, enter 1.

        1. Auto planning flag = 0, kanban is created but NOT planned.

        2. Auto planning flag = 1, kanban is created Planned.

        3. Auto planning flag >=2, quantity of kanbans accumulated prior to creating the kanbans as Planned.

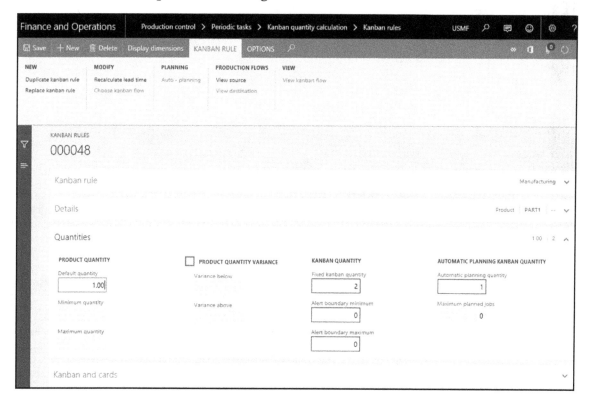

5.   On the Kanbans fast tab, click Add.

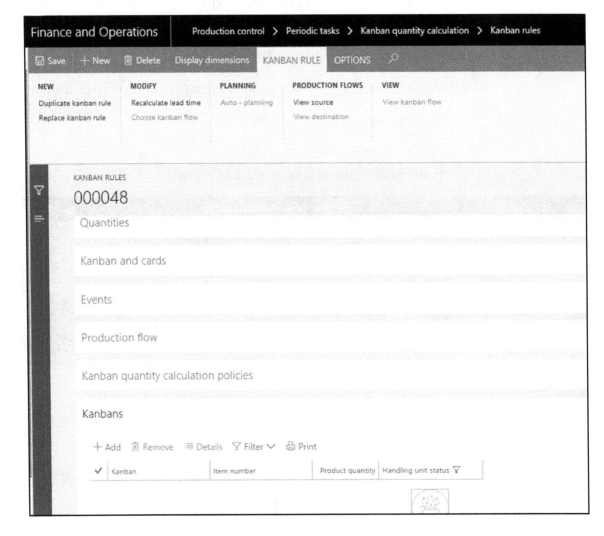

6. Apply number of kanbans. (will default to Quantities setting)

7. Click Create.

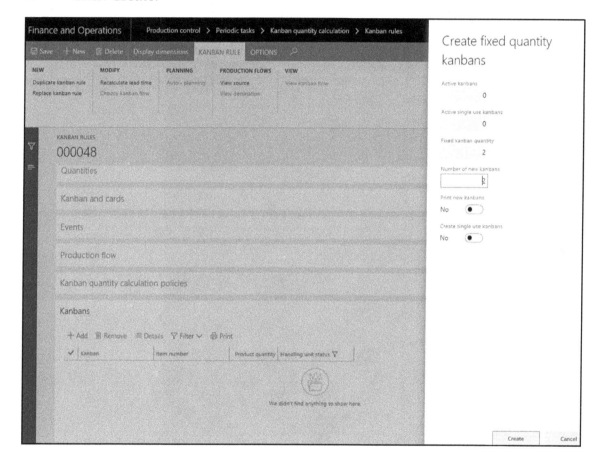

8. Click Save. Note number of non-circulating kanbans created. (to see job status, and/or cancel kanbans, click Details)

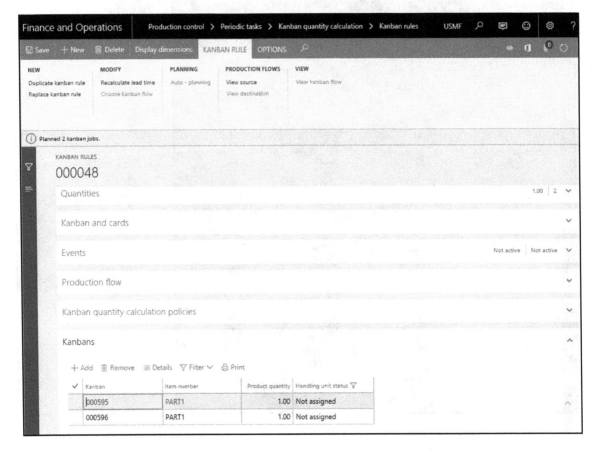

Kanban Rules - Fixed Circulating

Note: Instructions precede screen copies

1.   Click New.

    1.   Example uses manufacturing kanban, single activity.

2.   **Replenishment type defaults to Fixed**. In the First plan activity field, select a value.

    1.   Note, if using a multiple activity production flow, turn on the multiple activities flag and select the ending activity for multiple activity production flows. A Production Flow path is also defined via this setup step.

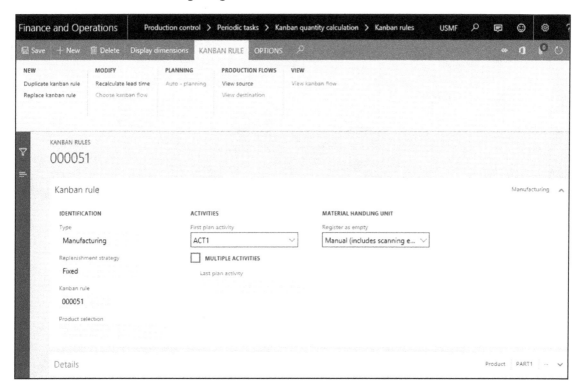

3. On the Details fast tab, in the Product field, apply a product.

   1. Product families are not used by Fixed

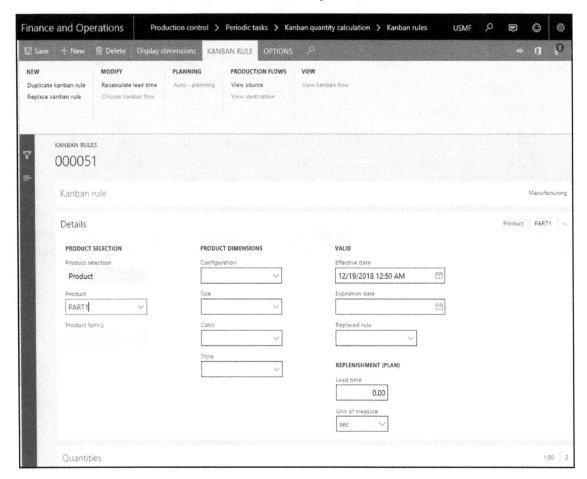

4.	On the Quantities fast tab, in the Default quantity field, enter a number.

5.	In the Fixed kanban (number of cards) quantity field, enter a number.

6.	In the Automatic planning quantity field, enter 1.

    1.	Auto planning flag = 0, kanban is created but NOT planned.

    2.	Auto planning flag = 1, kanban is created Planned.

    3.	Auto planning flag >=2, quantity of kanbans accumulated prior to creating the kanbans as Planned.

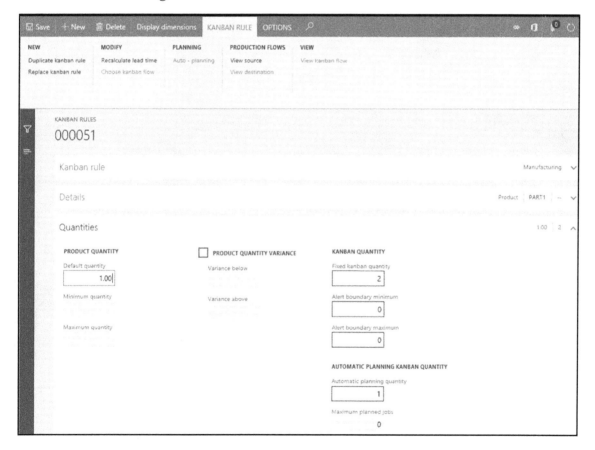

7. On the Kanban and Cards fast tab.

8. Select the Circulating cards check box.

9. In the Card assignment field, select an option. Automatic is the default.

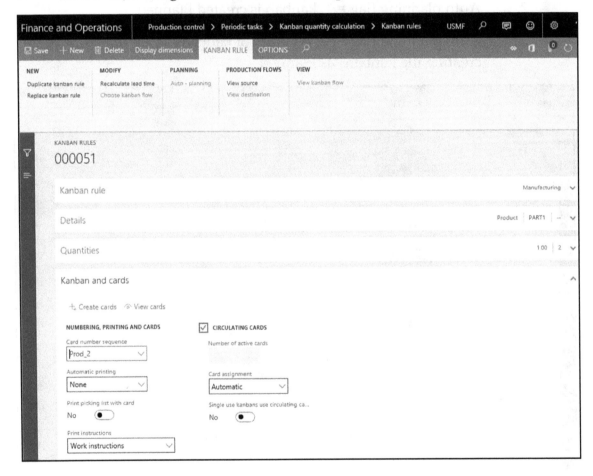

10. Click Create cards. (this process will be repeated on the kanbans fast tab)

11. Apply number of new cards. (will default to the Quantities setting)

12. Click Create.

    1. Note that the Print button is enabled

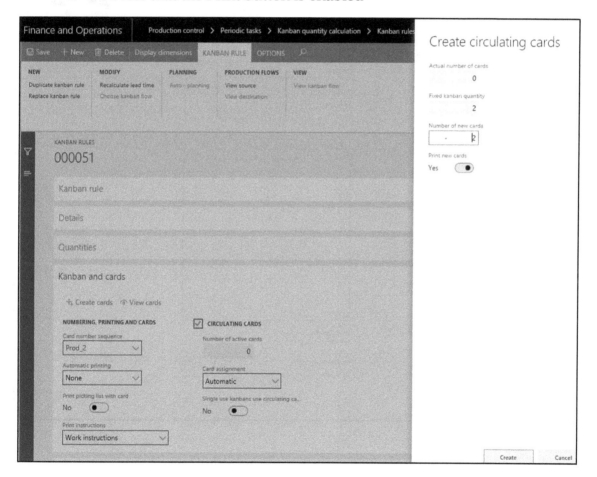

13. Close the page.

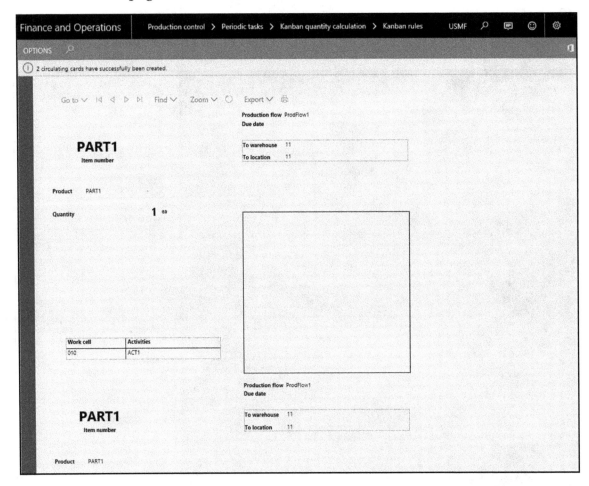

14.   On Kanbans fast tab click Add.

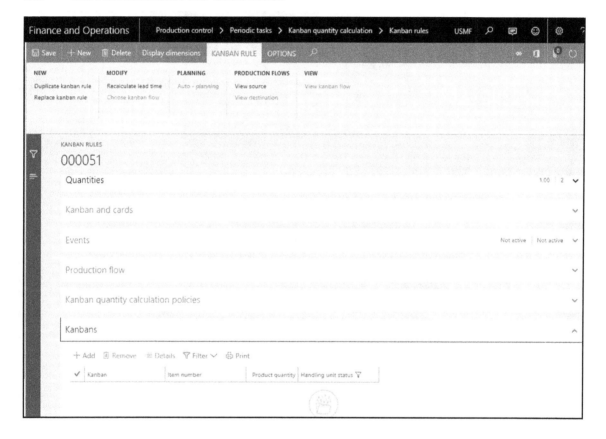

15. Apply number of new kanbans. (will default to Quantities setting)

16. Click Create.

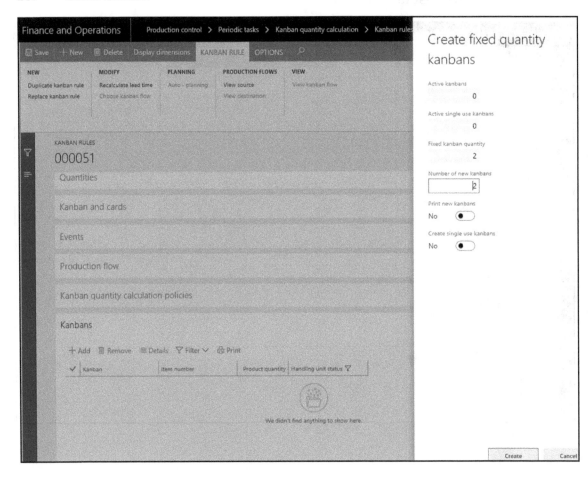

17. Click Add. Enter same number of cards as created above.

18. Note created cards. Kanban #'s are the same as those that can be seen in View Cards on the Kanban and Cards fast tab. #'s will be re-used when cards are emptied. (to see job status, and/or cancel kanbans, click Details)

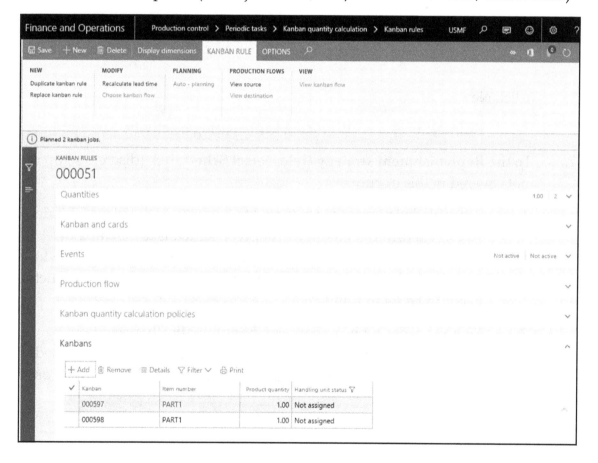

Kanban Rules - Scheduled

Note: Instructions precede screen copies

1. Click New.

    1. Example uses manufacturing kanban, single activity.

2. **In the Replenishment strategy field, select Scheduled**. (discrete setup is not covered in this document)

    1. Scheduled kanbans are converted to kanbans in the planned orders screen via firming. Planned order type kanbans are created by Master Planning using the relevant coverage setting applicable to the part. Note that the Default Order Setting on Released Products needs to be set to Kanban.

    2. Planned order type kanbans can be automatically firmed via coverage settings, and will create the kanban as either unplanned or planned via the automatic planning quantity that is defined on the kanban rule.

3.   In the First plan activity field, enter or select a value.

1.   Note, if a multiple activity production flow is used, turn on the
     multiple activities flag and select the ending activity for multiple
     activity production flows. A Production Flow path is also defined
     via this setup step.

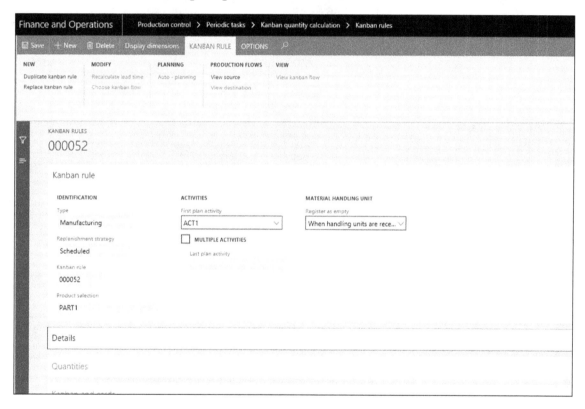

4.   On the Details fast tab, In the Product field, type or select a value.

       1.   Product families are enabled by selecting Product Families in the Product Selection field, and selecting an Item Allocation Key (used as a kanban rule group) in the Product Family field.

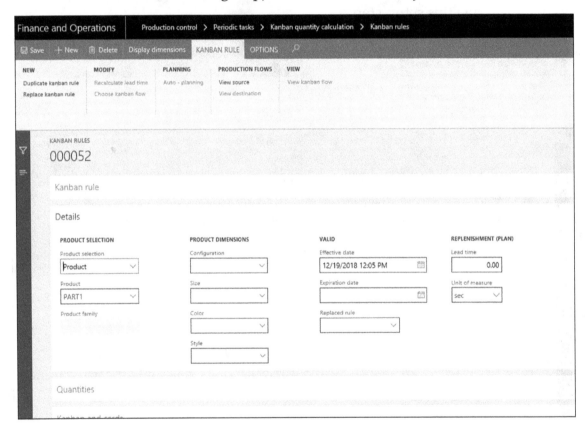

5. In the Default quantity field, enter a number.

6. In the Automatic planning quantity field, enter a number.

    1. Auto planning flag = 0, kanban is created, but NOT planned.

    2. Auto planning flag = 1, kanban is created Planned.

    3. Auto planning flag >=2, quantity of kanbans accumulated prior to creating the kanbans as Planned.

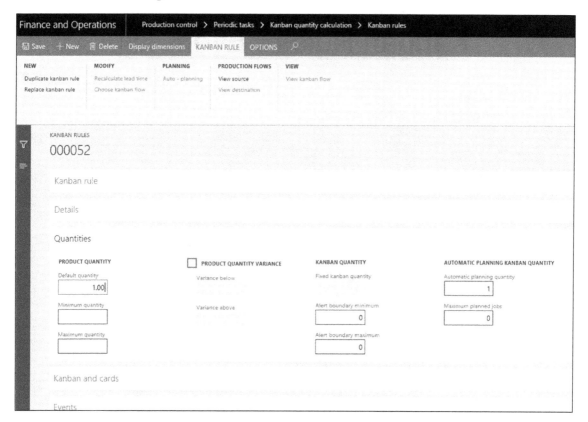

7. Click Save.

Kanban Rules - Event, all

Note: Instructions precede screen copies

1.   Click New.

     1.   Example uses manufacturing kanban, single activity.

2.   **In the Replenishment strategy field, select Event.**

3.   In the First plan activity field, enter or select a value.

   1.   Note, if using a multiple activity production flow, turn on the multiple activities flag and select the ending activity for multiple activity production flows. A Production Flow path is also defined via this setup step.

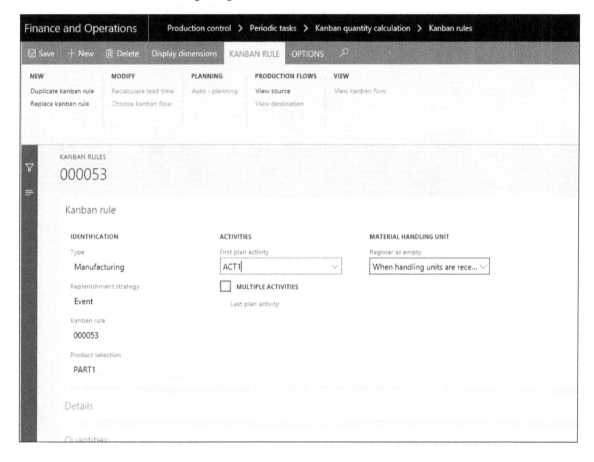

4.　On the Details fast tab, In the Product field, type or select a value.

　　1.　Product families are enabled by selecting Product Families in the Product Selection field, and selecting an Item Allocation Key (used as a kanban rule group) in the Product Family field.

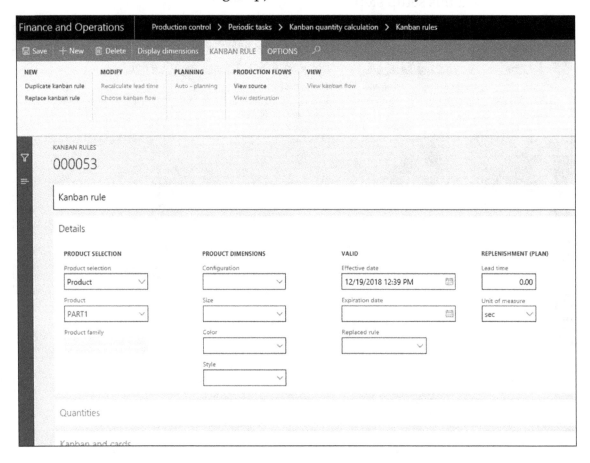

5.   In the Automatic planning quantity field, enter a number. (note, quantity is greyed out)

    1.   Auto planning flag = 0, kanban is created, but NOT planned.

    2.   Auto planning flag = 1, kanban is created Planned.

    3.   Auto planning flag >=2, quantity of kanbans accumulated prior to creating the kanbans as Planned.

6.   Note that the default quantity field is greyed out. Event kanban quantities are driven from the event type. Sales Events are MTO.

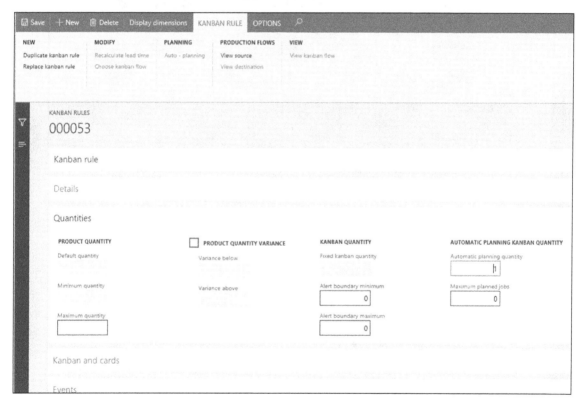

7. In the <u>Sales event</u> field, select an option and set to automatic.

8. **Other Event options:**

   1. <u>BOM Line event</u>: Generate kanban from a discrete production bill of material (discrete is not covered in this document)

   2. <u>Kanban Line event</u>: Generate kanban from a kanban (Note, requires chained production flows)

   3. <u>Stock Replenishment event</u>: Generate kanban from item coverage min (Note, not max)

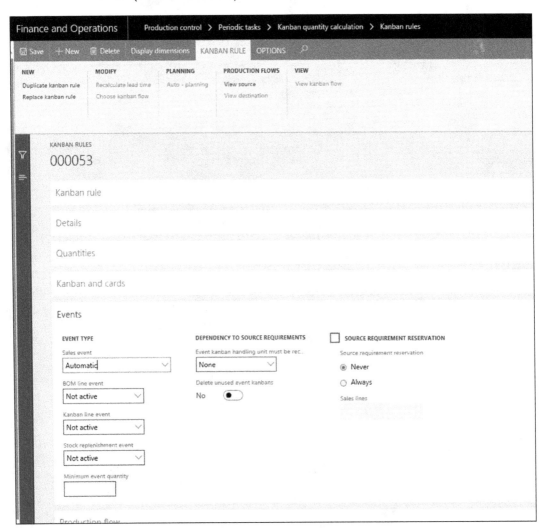

9.   Click Save.

10.   If any of the above are set to batch, set event processing under Kanban Job Batch Processing sub-menu.

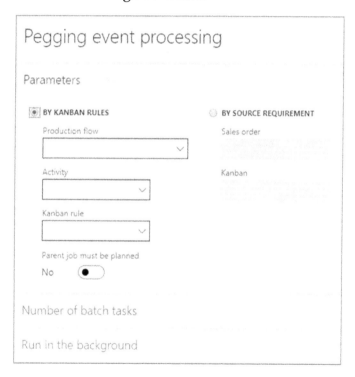

Kanban Rules - Withdrawal

Note: Instructions precede screen copies

1.   Click New.

2.   **In the Type field, select Withdrawal**. (defined as Transfer on Production Flow)

3.   In the First plan activity field, enter or select a value.

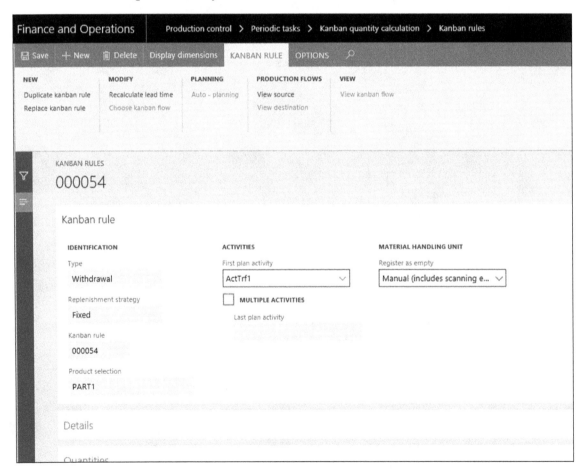

4. In the Product field, select a value.

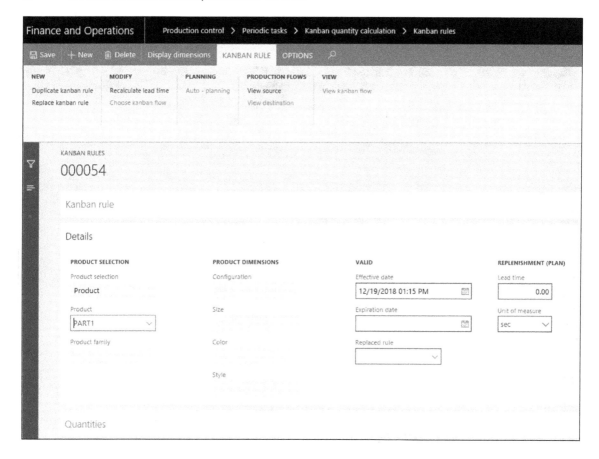

5. Enter quantities. (Note, example is fixed kanban)

   1. Note automatic planning field is greyed out. All transfer orders start unplanned.

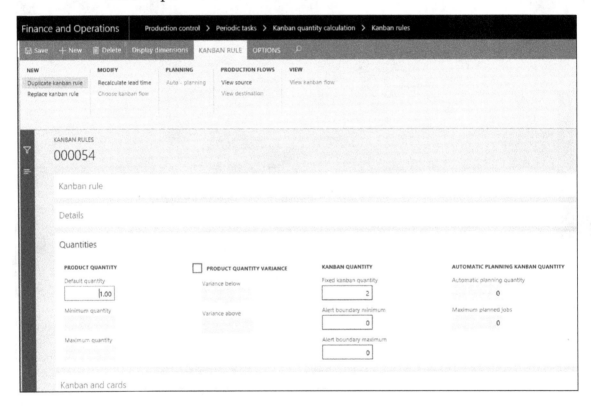

6.   Example is fixed kanban, requires card create, click Add

7.   Click Create.

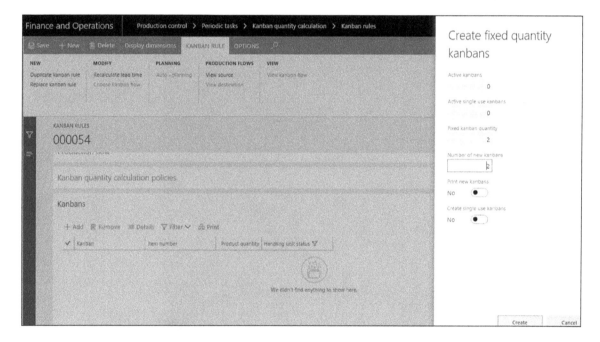

8.   Kanban creates are listed

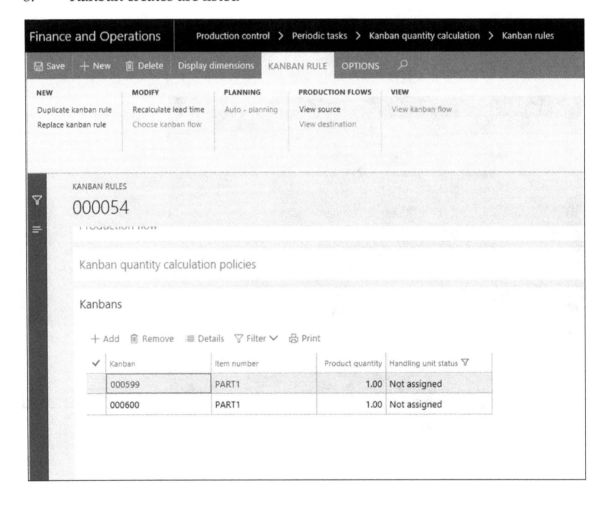

Kanban Schedule Board

Note: Instructions precede screen copies

Section Examples:

- Planned kanban schedule change.

- Planning an unplanned kanban.

1.   Go to Production control > Kanban > Kanban schedule board.

2.   Select work cell and 'view from' if applicable.

3.   Expand group

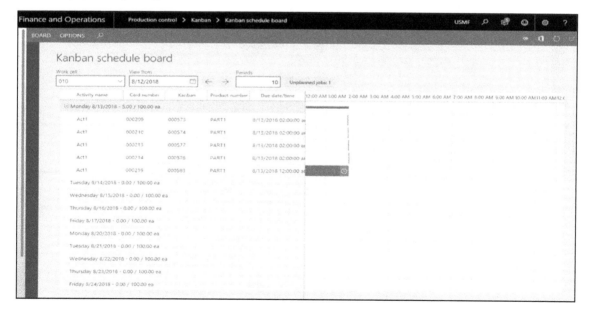

4.   Select activity. (in this example, activity time is changed to 1 hour from 5 minutes to highlight the transaction)

5.   Click Board action tab.

6.   In the Move sub-section click Next period.

7.   Click Start or End.

8.   Note kanban is moved to Tuesday.

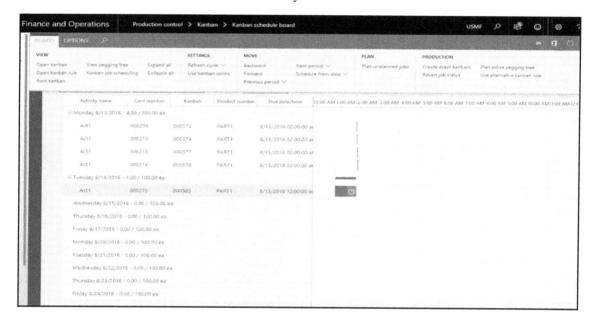

9.   Note # of unplanned jobs in header next to Periods.

10.   Click Board action tab.

11.   In the Plan sub-section click Plan unplanned jobs.

12. In the Period field, select a date.

13. Click OK.

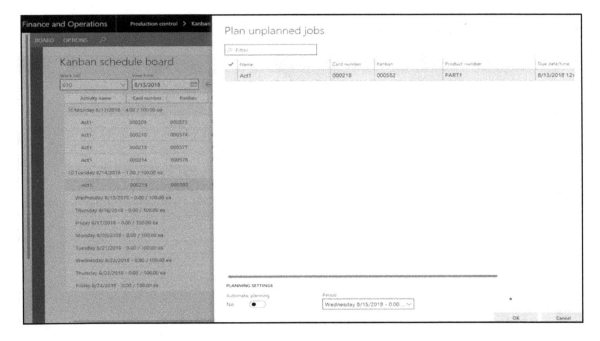

14. Note unplanned job is now planned.

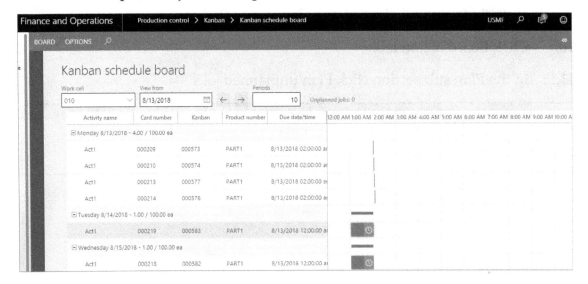

Kanban Board for Process Jobs

Note: Instructions precede screen copies

1. Go to Production control > Kanban > Kanban board for process jobs.

2. In the list, find and select the desired record.

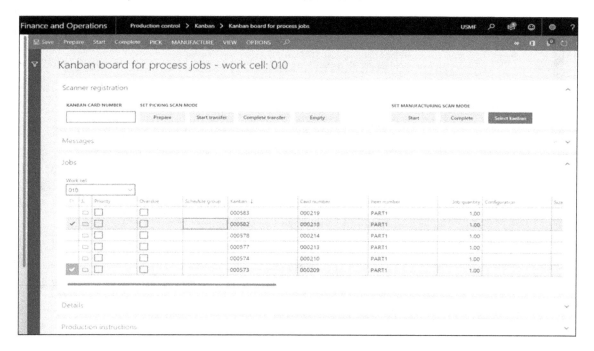

3. Click Prepare (from pull down at top), note job status.

Due date/time	Job status ↓	Work cell
8/13/2018 12:00:00 AM	Prepared	010

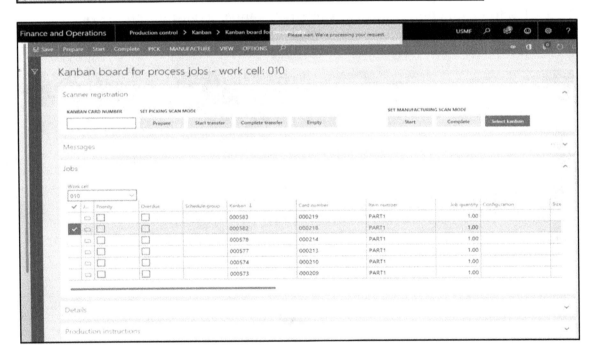

4.   Click Start (note Prepare is greyed out), note job status.

Due date/time	Job status ↓	Work cell
8/13/2018 12:00:00 AM	In progress	010

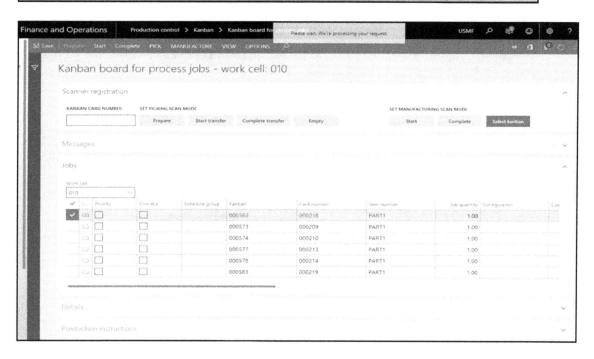

5.   Click Complete (note Start is greyed out), note job status.

Due date/time	Job status ↓	Work cell
8/13/2018 12:00:00 AM	Completed	010

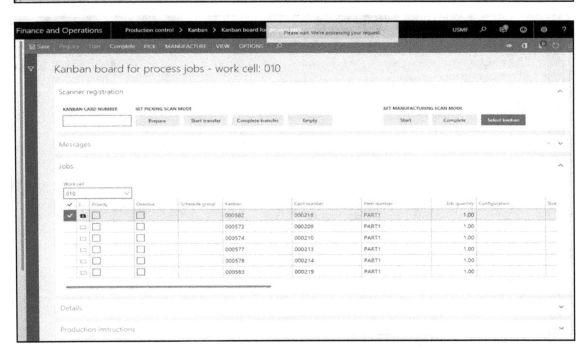

6.   Product is incremented in to inventory. (part is set to Site/Whse)

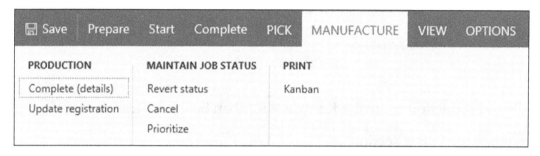

earch name	Site	Warehouse	Location	Physical inventory	Physical reserved	Available physical	Available physic...
PART1	1	11		1.00		1.00	1.00

7.   Note options available in Manufacture action tab.

🖫 Save	Prepare	Start	Complete	PICK	MANUFACTURE	VIEW	OPTIONS

PRODUCTION	MAINTAIN JOB STATUS	PRINT
Complete (details)	Revert status	Kanban
Update registration	Cancel	
	Prioritize	

8.   Note options available in View action tab.

    1.   Job Details filters will affect number of rows displayed.

🖫 Save	Prepare	Start	Complete	PICK	MANUFACTURE	VIEW	OPTIONS

SETTINGS	DIMENSIONS DISPLAY	KANBAN QUANTITY OVERVIEW
Refresh cycle ∨	Process job list	Finished goods
Job details ∨	Picking list and pegging	Materials
	Transfer job list	

9.   Note: any error messages will appear in Messages fast tab.

Messages		
✓	Message	Created date and time ↓

We didn't find anything to show here.

Kanban Board for Transfer Jobs

Note: Instructions precede screen copies

1. Go to Production control > Kanban > Kanban board for transfer jobs.

2. Update the Filters section.

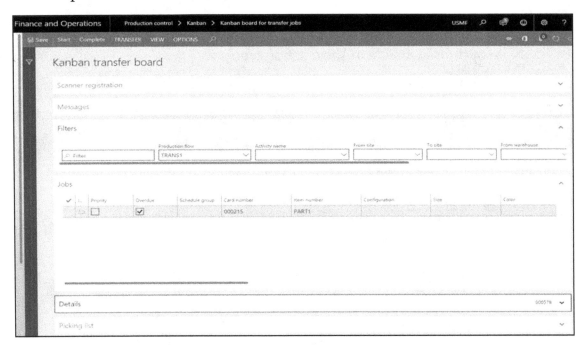

3. Click Start. (note status)

From warehouse	From location	To warehouse	To location	Dispatch date	Job status ↑
11	11	12	12		In progress

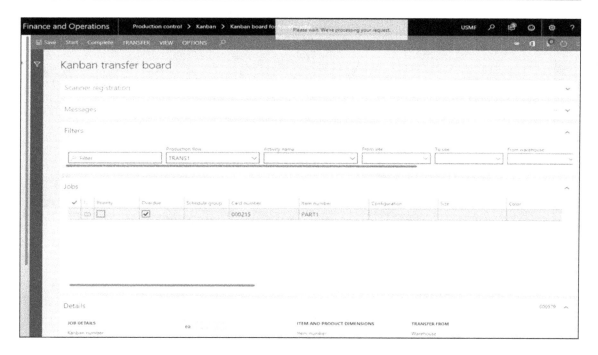

4.   Click Complete. (note status)

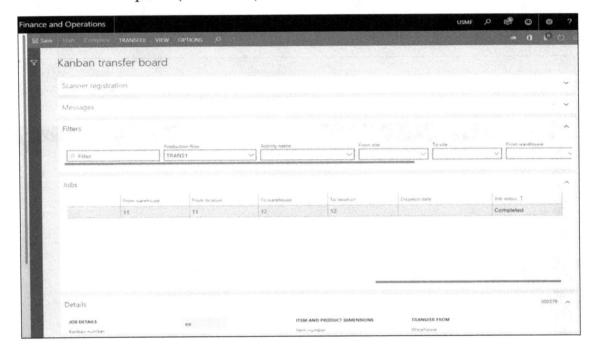

5.   Product is transferred.

Search name	Site	Warehouse	Location	Physical inventory	Physical reserved	Available physical	Available physic...
PART1	1	11					
PART1	1	12		1.00		1.00	1.00

ON-HAND : PART1 : PART1

Filter   Inventory quantities

NOTES

www.ingramcontent.com/pod-product-compliance
Lightning Source LLC
Chambersburg PA
CBHW060151060326
40690CB00018B/4074